ASPECTS
of PSYCHOLOGY ADOLESCENCE,

ton and Queen Elizabeth I Co

ASPECTS
of PSYCHOLOGY

ADOLESCENCE, ADULTHOOD and OLD AGE

ROB MCILVEEN & RICHARD GROSS

Hodder & Stoughton

A MEMBER OF THE HODDER HEADLINE GROUP

Dedication

To all students of Psychology: past, present and future

British Library Cataloguing in Publication Data
A catalogue record for this title is available from the British Library

ISBN 0 340 74896 6

First published 1999
Impression number 10 9 8 7 6 5 4 3 2 1
Year 2003 2002 2001 2000 1999

Copyright © 1999 Rob McIlveen and Richard Gross

Typeset by GreenGate Publishing Services, Tonbridge, Kent.
Printed and bound in Great Britain for Hodder and Stoughton Educational, a division of
Hodder Headline plc, 338 Euston Road, London NW1 3BH,
by Cox & Wyman, Reading, Berkshire

CONTENTS

The *Aspects of Psychology* series aims to provide a short and concise, but detailed and highly accessible, account of selected areas of psychological theory research.

Adolescence, Adulthood and Old Age consists of four chapters. Chapter 1 is concerned with personality change and social development in adolescence. Chapter 2 discusses theories of personality change in early and middle adulthood, whilst Chapter 3 considers the impact of critical life events(such as retirement and marriage) in adulthood. Chapter 4 focuses on late adulthood or old age, with discussion of major theories of adjustment to this final period of the life cycle.

For the purposes of revision, we have included detailed summaries of the material presented in each chapter. Instead of a separate glossary, for easy reference the Index contains page numbers in **bold** which refer to definitions and main explanations of particular concepts.

ACKNOWLEDGEMENTS

We would like to thank Dave Mackin, Anna Churchman and Denise Stewart at GreenGate Publishing for their swift and efficient preparation of the text. Thanks also to Greig Aitken at Hodder for all his hard work in coordinating this project (we hope it's the first of many!), and to Tim Gregson-Williams for his usual help and support.

The publishers would like to thank the following for permission to reproduce photographs and other illustrations in this book:

p.2 (Fig 1.1), The Kobal Collection; p.4 (Fig 1.2), Castlemead Publications; p.16 (Fig 1.3), Routledge, from Coleman J.C. and Hendry L. *The Nature of Adolescence*, Second Edition, published 1990 by Routledge; p.25 (Fig 2.1), BBC Worldwide Ltd; p.31 (Fig 2.3), The Ronald Grant Archive; p.35 (Fig 2.4), The McGraw-Hill Companies from *Psychology*, Fifth Edition by Santrock, J. *et al.*, copyright 1997 The McGraw-Hill Companies reproduced by permission of the publishers; p.44 (Fig 3.1), BBC Worldwide Ltd; p.50 (Fig 3.2), Sally and Richard Greenhill Kate Mayers; p.56 (Fig 3.3), Sally and Richard Greenhill © Kate Mayers; p.66 (Fig 4.2), Times Newspapers Limited © Peter Brookes/The Times, 1996; p.71 (Fig 4.3) (top), Topham Picture Point; (bottom) Sally and Richard Greenhill.

Every effort has been made to obtain necessary permission with reference to copyright material. The publishers apologise if inadvertently any sources remain unacknowledged and will be glad to make the necessary arrangements at the earliest opportunity.

PERSONALITY CHANGE AND SOCIAL DEVELOPMENT IN ADOLESCENCE

Introduction and overview

The word 'adolescence' comes from the Latin *adolescere* meaning 'to grow into maturity'. As well as being a time of enormous physiological change, adolescence is also marked by changes in behaviour and expectations. Traditionally, adolescence has been regarded as a prelude to and preparation for adulthood, a transitional period of life between immaturity and maturity. Although there is no single initiation rite in our society that signals the passage into adulthood, there are a number of important 'marker' events, such as leaving school or college, obtaining a job, or moving out of the family home.

In Western societies, adolescence typically spans the ages 12 to 20 which, by other cultures' standards, is unusually long. Indeed, in some non-industrialised societies, adolescence is either virtually non-existent or simply a period of rapid physical changes leading to maturity.

This chapter examines several theories and associated research into personality change and social development in adolescence. Emphasis will be given to the theories of Hall, Erikson, Marcia and Coleman, and sociological (or social psychological) approaches. It begins by looking at the concept of adolescence.

The concept of adolescence

Adolescence is usually taken to begin at *puberty*, the period when sexual maturation begins. Puberty typically begins about two years later for boys than for girls (Chumlea, 1982). However, whilst ten and 12 are the ages by which most girls and boys respectively have entered puberty, there are considerable individual differences. There are also *secular growth trends* (differences between *cultures* in the age at which puberty begins). In some cultures, the age at which puberty begins has been *declining* (Hamburg & Takanishi, 1989). Improvements in nourishment and health care are at least partly responsible for the observed secular growth trends.

Box 1.1 *Major changes in puberty*

Physiologically, puberty begins when the seminal vesicles and prostate gland enlarge in the male, and the ovaries enlarge in the female. Both males and females experience the *adolescent growth spurt*. Male *secondary sex characteristics* include growth of pubic and then chest and facial hair, and sperm production (see Figure 1.1a). In females, breast size increases, pubic hair grows, and menstruation begins (see Figure 1.1b, opposite).

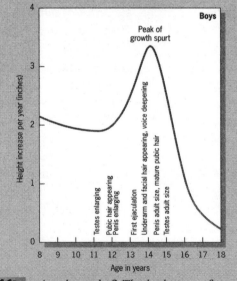

Figure 1.1a *(see also overleaf) The development of secondary sex characteristics in boys. The curved lines represent the average increase in height from eight to 18 years of age. The characteristics shown may occur earlier or later in a person's development but usually occur in the order shown (Based on Tanner, 1978, and Tanner & Whitehouse, 1976)*

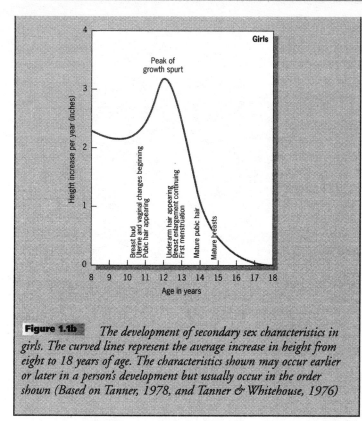

Figure 1.1b *The development of secondary sex characteristics in girls. The curved lines represent the average increase in height from eight to 18 years of age. The characteristics shown may occur earlier or later in a person's development but usually occur in the order shown (Based on Tanner, 1978, and Tanner & Whitehouse, 1976)*

Given the considerable variation in the timing of these physical changes, it is difficult to define adolescence in terms of *chronological age* (such as 'the teenage years'). Indeed, some researchers maintain that adolescence is difficult to define because it has been *artificially created* by Western culture and is a recent 'invention' of Western capitalist society. For example, it has been argued that the concept of the 'rebellious teenager' is a relatively recent phenomenon, popularised in the 1950s through films like *Rebel Without A Cause*. However, the 2000-year-old writings of the ancient Greek philosopher Plato illustrate how the young were seen as being the most likely to challenge the existing social order (Coleman, 1995). Furthermore, Montemayor's (1983) analysis of parent–adolescent relationships from the 1920s to the 1980s, shows that both the issues over which disagreement occurred and the overall levels of conflict were extremely similar.

Figure 1.2 *1950s films such as* Rebel Without A Cause, *starring James Dean, have been seen as helping to create the concept of the 'rebellious teenager'. However, Plato was writing about youth's challenge to the existing social order more than 2000 years ago*

Montemayor's research indicates that adolescence has changed very little in the twentieth century, despite enormous social and economic changes. Although the term 'teenager' came into existence only in 1953, adolescence has been in existence for very much longer and has probably manifested itself differently according to culture and historical context. However, *some* form of transitional change is common to most societies, suggesting that adolescence is not an invention of Western capitalist society (Coleman, 1995).

The 'classical' view of adolescence proposes three main components: *storm and stress, identity crisis* and the *generation gap.* Several theories have, in various ways, contributed to this classical view.

Hall's theory

This is probably the earliest formal theory of adolescence. Influenced by Darwin's evolutionary theory, Hall (1904) believed that each person's psychological development *recapitulates* (or recaptures) both the biological and cultural evolution of the human species. He saw adolescence as a time of 'storm and stress' (or *Sturm und Drang*), which mirrored the volatile history of the human race over the last 2000 years.

Some evidence suggests that reactions are more *intense* during adolescence than any other period of life, and that adolescence can be a 'difficult' phase, at least for parents. The National Children's Bureau study, for example, looked at over 14,000 16-year-olds born in a single week in 1958 in England, Scotland and Wales (Fogelman, 1976). Parents most often described their adolescent children as solitary, irritable ('quick to fly off the handle') or 'fussy and overparticular'.

Box 1.2 *Csikszentmihalyi & Larson's (1984) study of adolescent reactions*

Seventy-five Chicago-area high-school students from diverse social and racial backgrounds were asked to wear electronic pagers for a week. Every two hours, the pager signalled to the students who were instructed to write a description of what they were doing and how they felt about it. After a week, the students filled out questionnaires about both their general moods and their specific mood during particular activities. About 40 per cent of waking time was spent pursuing leisure activities, such as socialising with friends, playing sport or just 'thinking'. The other 60 per cent was spent roughly equally in 'maintenance activities' (such as commuting and eating) and 'productive activities' (such as studying and working).

Particularly revealing were the extreme mood swings. Csikszentmihalyi and Larson found that the students swung from extreme happiness to deep sadness (and vice versa) in less than an hour. For adults, such mood swings usually require several hours to reach the same emotional peaks and troughs.

Although adolescence can be a difficult time of life, little evidence supports Hall's contention that it is a period of storm and stress, and much rejects it. For example, amongst families of middle class American adolescents, adolescence is no more stressful than childhood or adulthood (Bandura & Walters, 1959). British research has reached the same conclusion. Rutter *et al.* (1976) found only small differences between the number of ten-year-olds (10.9 per cent), 14-year-olds (12.5 per cent) and adults (11.9 per cent) judged as having mental disorders. Moreover, a large proportion of 14-year-olds with disorders had had them since childhood. When difficulties did first appear during adolescence, they were mainly associated with stressful situations such as parents' marital discord.

Likewise, Siddique & D'Arcy (1984) found that over a third of adolescents reported no symptoms of psychological distress, and around 40 per cent reported only mild levels. So, whilst adolescence may be a period of stress and turmoil for some, the vast majority adjust well to this transitional phase. For Offer (1969), this vast majority possess egos strong enough to withstand the pressures of that phase of life. Because they are in touch with their feelings, and develop meaningful relationships with significant others, they do not experience the turmoil of the disturbed adolescent.

Erikson's theory

Along with Adler (1927), Erikson (1963) was one of the first to challenge the view that personality development stops in childhood. Erikson believed that there is a fixed and pre-determined sequence of stages in human development. His *epigenetic principle* maintains that the entire pattern of social and psychological growth is governed by a genetic structure common to all humans, in which genes dictate a timetable for development. It is human nature to pass through a genetically determined sequence of *psychosocial stages*.

Erikson saw the sequence of stages as being *universal*. However, he also saw the sociocultural environment as having a significant influence on our dominant modes of acting and thinking. Based on observations of patients in his psychoanalytic practice, Erikson proposed eight psychosocial stages, each of which centres around a crisis involving a struggle between two conflicting personality outcomes. One of these outcomes is positive (or *adaptive*) whilst the other is negative (or *maladaptive*). Erikson did not, however, see these as either/or alternatives. Rather, every personality is a mixture of the two: healthy development involves the adaptive outweighing the maladaptive (see Table 1.1, page 9).

The major challenges of adolescence represent the fifth of Erikson's eight psychosocial stages, in which the individual must face the crisis of establishing a strong sense of personal identity. The dramatic onset of puberty, combined with more sophisticated intellectual abilities, results in adolescents becoming particularly concerned with finding their own personal place in adult society. It also results in a lengthy and sometimes painful process of assessing particular strengths and weaknesses so that realistic goals can be set.

Western societies, at least, see adolescence as a *moratorium*, an authorised delay of adulthood, which frees adolescents from most responsibilities and helps them make the difficult transition from childhood to adulthood. Although this can be helpful, it can also be extremely unhelpful. For example, although adolescents may still be dependent on adults, they are expected to behave in an independent and adult way. Thus, the question 'When do I become an adult?' elicits a response from a teacher which is different from a doctor's, parent's or police officer's (Coleman, 1995).

As well as having to deal with the question 'Who am I?', the adolescent must also deal with the question 'Who will I be?'. Erikson saw the creation of an adult personality as accomplished mainly through choosing and developing a commitment to an occupation or role in life. The development of *ego identity* (a firm sense of who one is and what one stands for) is positive, and can carry people through difficult times. For some, however, the need to achieve their potential and create the best possible life is contrasted with the concern to remain true to their ideals. When working with psychiatrically disturbed soldiers in World War II, Erikson coined the term *identity crisis* to describe the loss of personal identity which the stress of combat seemed to have caused. Some years later, he extended the use of the term to include:

'severely conflicted young people whose sense of confusion is due ... to a war within themselves'.

Failure to integrate perceptions of the self into a coherent whole results in *role confusion*. According to Erikson, role confusion can take several forms. Sometimes it is shown in an aimless drifting through a series of social and occupational roles. However, the consequences can be more severe, leading the adolescent into abnormal or delinquent behaviour (such as drug taking and even suicide). Erikson calls this type of role confusion *negative identity*, the choice of adolescents who, because they cannot resolve their identity crises, adopt extreme positions that set them aside from the crowd. For someone with negative identity, the extreme position is preferable to the loneliness and isolation that come with failing to achieve a distinct and more functional role in life.

Table 1.1   *Erikson's eight psychosocial stages of development*

Stage	Personal/ social relationships	Crisis or conflict	Possible outcome
Birth to 1 year	Mother	Trust vs. mistrust	Trust and faith in others or a mistrust of people
2 years	Parents	Autonomy vs. shame and doubt	Self-control and mastery or self-doubt and fearfulness
3 to 5 years	Family	Initiative vs. guilt	Purpose and direction or a loss of self-esteem
6 to 11 years	Neighbourhood and school	Industry vs. inferiority	Competence in social and intellectual pursuits or a failure to thrive and develop
Adolescence	Peer groups and outgroups; models of leadership	Identity vs. role confusion	A sense of 'who one is' or prolonged uncertainty about one's role in life
Early adulthood	Partners, in friendship sex, competition, co-operation	Intimacy vs isolation	Formation of deep personal relationships or the failure to love others
Middle age	Divided labour and shared household	Generativity vs. stagnation	Expansion of interests and caring for others or a turning inward toward one's own problems
Old age	'Mankind', 'My kind'	Integrity vs. despair	Satisfaction with the triumphs and disappointments of life or a sense of unfulfilment and a fear of death

(After Erikson, 1963)

Box 1.3 *Three other major forms of role confusion*

Intimacy: This is a fear of commitment to, or involvement in, close relationships, arising from a fear of losing one's own identity. The result of this may be stereotyped and formalised relationships or isolation.

Time perspective: This is the inability to plan for the future or retain any sense of time. It is associated with anxieties about change and becoming an adult.

Industry: This is a difficulty in channelling resources in a realistic way in work or study, both of which require commitment. As a defence, the adolescent may find it impossible to concentrate, or become frenetically engaged in a single activity to the exclusion of all others.

Tests of Erikson's theory have typically used measures of the self-concept (especially *self-esteem*) as indicators of crisis. Simmons & Rosenberg (1975) have shown that, especially in girls, low self-esteem is more common during early adolescence than in either late childhood or later adolescence. However, in general, there is no increase in the disturbance of the self-image during early adolescence (Offer *et al.*, 1988). For Coleman & Hendry (1990), such disturbance is more likely in early than late adolescence (especially around puberty), but only a very small proportion of the total adolescent population is likely to have a negative self-image or very low self-esteem.

Erikson's theory has also been criticised on the grounds that it is based on observations of a restricted group of people (largely middle class, white males). Gilligan (1982) has argued that Erikson's theory is applicable only to males. Whilst it might be true that male adolescents want to forge a separate identity, Gilligan argues that females are more interested in developing warm and nurturing relationships and less interested in the idea of separateness. For Gilligan, Erikson is guilty of taking the male experience as the standard (*androcentrism*) and applying this to both men and women.

Marcia's theory

In an extension of Erikson's work, Marcia (1980) defines identity as:

'A self structure – an internal, self-constructed, dynamic organisation of drive, abilities, beliefs and individual history. The better developed this structure is, the more aware individuals appear to be of their own uniqueness and similarity to others and of their strengths and weaknesses in making their way in the world.'

Marcia identified four *statuses* of adolescent identity formation which characterise the search for identity. A mature identity can only be achieved if an individual experiences several *crises* in exploring and choosing between life's alternatives, finally arriving at a *commitment* or investment of the self in those choices.

Box 1.4 *Marcia's four statuses*

(Note that the *Associated occupational commitment* is a hypothetical response to the question 'How willing do you think you'd be to give up going into an occupation if something better were to come along?')

Identity diffusion: The individual is in crisis and unable to formulate clear self-definition, goals and commitments. This represents an inability to 'take hold' of some kind of adult identity.
Associated occupational commitment: 'Sounds like a good idea. I haven't thought about it, but I'll try everything once. I could switch just like that.' (snapping his fingers).

Identity foreclosure: The individual has avoided the uncertainties and anxieties of crisis by rapidly committing him- or herself to safe and conventional goals without exploring the many options open.
Associated occupational commitment: 'I doubt I'd be willing. I've always known what I wanted to do. My parents have agreed, and we're happy with it.'

Identity moratorium: Decisions about identity are postponed while the individual tries out alternative identities without being committed to any particular one.
Associated occupational commitment: 'It's possible. I kind of like a couple of fields – and if something else was related, I'd want to think about it and get some information.'

> **Identity achievement:** The individual has experienced a crisis but has emerged successfully with firm commitments, goals and ideology.
> *Associated occupational commitment:* 'I've given it a lot of thought. If I could see that there might be something better, I'd consider it.'
> **(From Gross, 1996, and Sarafino & Armstrong, 1980)**

According to Marcia, identity moratorium is a prerequisite for identity achievement. Beyond that, however, he does not see the four *statuses* as being sequential, which means that they are not Erikson-type stages. However, evidence suggests that, amongst 12- to 24-year-old men, the statuses *are* broadly age-related. Meilman (1979), for example, has reported that younger men (aged 12 to 18) were more likely to experience diffusion or foreclosure, whereas older men were increasingly likely to be identity achievers. However, irrespective of age, relatively few men were achieving moratorium. Since Marcia sees moratorium as the peak of crisis, Meilman's data cast doubt on the validity of the four statuses. Meilman's study, though, is cross-sectional. Several *longitudinal* studies have indicated clear patterns of movement from foreclosure and diffusion to moratorium and achievement statuses (Kroger, 1996). However, when applied to females, even Marcia (1980) accepts that his statuses work 'only more or less'. This is another example of androcentrism.

A sociological (or social psychological) theory

Sociologists see *role change* as an integral feature of adolescent development (Coleman, 1995). Changing school or college, leaving home and beginning a job, all involve a new set of relationships, producing different and often greater expectations. These expectations themselves demand a substantial reassessment of the self-concept and *speed up* the socialisation process. Some adolescents find this problematic because of the wide variety of competing socialisation agencies (such as the family, mass media and peer group) which often represent *conflicting* values and demands.

Sociologists also see socialisation as being dependent more on the adolescent's *own generation* than on the family or other social institutions (*auto-socialisation*: Marsland, 1987). As Marsland has observed:

'The crucial meaning of youth is withdrawal from adult control and influence compared with childhood. Peer groups are the milieu into which young people withdraw … this withdrawal … is, within limits, legitimated by the adult world'.

Marsland is describing *the generation gap*. However, there is considerable evidence of *good* relationships between the vast majority of parents and their adolescent children.

Of course, it is almost inevitable that there should be conflict between parents and their adolescent children. Adolescents could not grow into adults unless they were able to test out the boundaries of authority, and they could not discover their beliefs unless given the opportunity to push hard against other people's (Coleman, 1995). However, little evidence supports the extreme view that whatever generation gap exists leads to a 'war' between the generations or the formation of an adolescent subculture. For example, Offer *et al.* (1988) found that over 91 per cent of adolescents in nine different cultures (including Bangladesh, Turkey and Taiwan) denied holding grudges against their parents. A similar percentage rejected the idea that their parents were ashamed of them or would be disappointed in them in the future.

Box 1.5 *Is there a generation gap?*

- Bandura & Walters (1959) found that the typical American adolescent tended to accept most parental values quite freely and associated with other adolescents who shared such values.
- In the National Children's Bureau study (Fogelman, 1976), parents were given a list of issues on which it is commonly believed that they and their 16-year-old adolescent children disagree. As Tables 1.2 and 1.3 illustrate, parents saw their relationships with their adolescent children as being harmonious, a view confirmed by their children. The only major disagreements concerned appearance and evening activities.
- Other research (e.g. Noller & Callan, 1990) indicates that music, fashion and sexual behaviour tend to be the issues on which a sizeable 'generation gap' appears.

Table 1.2 *Percentage of parents reporting disagreement with their adolescent children (N = 11,521)*

	Often (%)	Sometimes (%)	Never or hardly ever (%)
Choice of same-sex friends	3	16	81
Choice of opposite-sex friends	2	9	89
Dress or hairstyle	11	35	54
Time of coming in at night or going to bed	8	26	66
Places visited in own time	2	9	89
Doing homework	6	18	76
Smoking	6	9	85
Drinking	1	5	94

(From the National Children's Bureau study: Fogelman, 1976)

Table 1.3 *Reports by adolescents concerning their parents (N = 11,045)*					
	Very true (%)	**True (%)**	**Uncertain (%)**	**Untrue (%)**	**Very untrue (%)**
I get on well with my mother	41	45	8	4	1
I get on well with my father	35	45	13	5	2
I often quarrel with a sister or brother	23	43	10	19	5
My parents have strong views about my appearance	15	33	19	27	6
My parents want to know where I go in the evening	27	51	8	11	3
My parents disapprove of some of my male friends	9	19	18	37	16
My parents disapprove of some of my female friends	5	15	18	40	22

(From the National Children's Bureau study: Fogelman, 1976)

Coleman's focal theory

According to Coleman & Hendry (1990), the theories above are relevant and provide a foundation for an understanding of young people with serious problems and those who belong to minority or deviant groups. However, adolescence requires a theory of *normality* rather than *abnormality*. The transition from childhood to adolescence requires substantial psychological and social adjustment. Whilst adolescence is a difficult time for some, for the majority it appears to be a period of relative stability with which most young people cope without undue stress. Coleman's (1980) *focal theory* is an attempt to explain how this is achieved.

The theory is based on a study of 800 six-, 11-, 13-, 15- and 17-year-old boys and girls. Coleman found that on various tests dealing with self-image, being alone, heterosexual and parental relationships, and friendships and large-group situations, attitudes to all of these changed as a function of age. More important, though, was the finding that concerns about different issues reached a peak at different ages for both sexes.

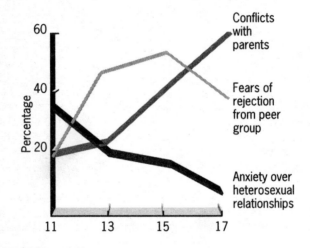

Figure 1.3　　*Peak ages of the expression of different themes. These data are for boys only (From Coleman & Hendry, 1990)*

Particular sorts of relationship patterns come into *focus* (are most prominent) at different ages. However, no pattern is specific to one age. The patterns overlap and there are wide individual differences with respect to them, but just because an issue is not the predominant feature of an age does not mean it will not be critical for some adolescents. Coleman believes that adolescents are able to cope with the potentially stressful change with relative stability by dealing with one issue at a time.

Thus, adolescents spread the process of adaptation over a span of years, attempting to resolve one issue first before addressing the next. Because different problems and relationships come into focus and are dealt with at different stages, the stresses resulting from the need to adapt are rarely concentrated so that all must be dealt with at once. Adolescents who, for whatever reason, must deal with more than one problem at a time, are those most likely to experience difficulties (Coleman & Hendry, 1990).

Box 1.6   *How valid is Coleman's theory?*

Coleman's original findings concerning patterns of development have been successfully replicated by Kroger (1985) with large North American and New Zealand samples. Others (e.g. Simmons & Blyth, 1987) have successfully tested hypotheses deriving from Coleman's theory. Simmons and Blyth proposed that those who adjust less well during adolescence would be more likely to be those facing more than one interpersonal issue at a time. Their results strongly supported the prediction. So, if change occurred at too young an age (causing the individual to be 'off-time' in development), was marked by sharp discontinuity, or involved an accumulation of significant and temporally close changes, adjustment was much poorer. Whilst Coleman's theory needs further testing, it is widely accepted as an important contribution to the understanding of adolescence.

Conclusions

This chapter has looked at several theoretical accounts of personality change and social development in adolescence. Although adolescence is 'classically' seen as a period of 'storm and stress' in which an adolescent experiences an 'identity crisis', and the 'generation gap' is at its widest, evidence does not favour such a view. The theories that have contributed to this classical view are probably furthest away from capturing the essence of adolescence.

Summary

- 'Adolescence' means 'to grow into maturity'. It spans the ages 12 to 20 and involves enormous changes in physiology, behaviour and expectations, a transitional period between immaturity and maturity. However, in some non-industrialised societies, adolescence either does not exist or simply denotes a period of rapid physical changes.

- Adolescence is usually taken to begin at **puberty**. Both sexes experience the **adolescent growth spurt** and the development of **secondary sex characteristics**. Girls typically begin puberty earlier than boys, but there are large individual differences within each sex. There are also **secular growth trends**.

- Some researchers see adolescence as a recent and **artificially created** stage in human development within Western capitalist society. However, adolescence has changed very little for much of the twentieth century, despite enormous social and economic changes. Some transitional period is found in most societies.

- Several theories have contributed to the 'classical' view of adolescence, which comprises '**storm and stress**', '**identity crisis**' and the '**generation gap**'.

- According to Hall, each person's psychological development **recapitulates** both the biological and cultural evolution of humans. Adolescence is a time of 'storm and stress' ('Sturm und Drang'), mirroring the human race's volatile history over the last 2000 years.

- Emotional reactions are more **intense** during adolescence compared with other periods of life, making it a 'difficult' time, at least for parents. Nevertheless, evidence suggests that adolescence is no more stressful than childhood or adulthood, and the rate of mental disorder is no greater for adolescents.

- According to Erikson's **epigenetic principle**, there is a fixed, pre-determined sequence of social and psychological development. It is human nature to pass through a genetically determined sequence of **psychosocial stages**.

- During adolescence, the individual faces a crisis centred on establishing a strong sense of personal identity (**identity** vs. **role confusion**). In Western societies, adolescence is a **moratorium**, designed to help individuals make the difficult transition from childhood to adulthood. This can be confusing, because 'adult' is defined differently by different social institutions.

- The creation of an adult personality (**ego-identity**) is achieved mainly through commitment to an occupational role. **Role confusion** can take the form of aimless drifting through a series of social and occupational roles. Alternatively, an adolescent may adopt a **negative identity**, as in delinquent behaviour. Three other forms of role confusion relate to **intimacy**, **time perspective** and **industry**.

- Although low self-esteem (a measure of **identity crisis**) may be more common in early adolescence (especially in girls), only a very small proportion of all adolescents have a disturbed self-image. Erikson's theory is also based largely on observations of white, middle class males, making it androcentric.

- Marcia identifies four **statuses** of adolescent **identity formation**: **identity diffusion**, **identity foreclosure**, **identity moratorium** and **identity achievement**. A mature identity can only be achieved if an individual experiences several **crises** before arriving at a **commitment** to certain choices.

- Whilst identity moratorium is a prerequisite for identity achievement, Marcia's four statuses are not sequential stages. Supporting evidence is based on male samples and the four statuses apply only loosely to females.

- For sociologists, adolescent development involves **role change**, requiring a substantial reassessment of the self-concept and **speeding up** of the socialisation process. Some adolescents find this difficult, because a wide range of socialisation agencies often present conflicting values and demands.

- Sociologists also stress **auto-socialisation**. However, most evidence shows adolescents sharing their parents' values, attitudes and beliefs, and the existence of harmonious family relationships.
- Some degree of conflict between parents and their adolescent children is necessary for adolescents to grow into adults. However, this is very different from claiming that there is a **generation gap** or that a separate adolescent sub-culture exists.
- Coleman's **focal theory** attempts to explain the **normality** of adolescents. Concerns about different issues reach a peak at different ages for both sexes. Adolescents cope with change by dealing with one issue at a time, spreading the process of adaptation over several years. Those who must deal with more than one issue at once are most likely to experience difficulties.

PERSONALITY CHANGE IN EARLY AND MIDDLE ADULTHOOD

2

Introduction and overview

Assuming we enjoy a normal life-span, the longest phase of the life-cycle will be spent in adulthood. Until recently, however, personality changes in adulthood attracted little psychological research interest. Indeed, as Levinson *et al.* (1978) have observed, adulthood is:

> 'one of the best-kept secrets in our society and probably in human history generally'.

This chapter attempts to reveal some of these secrets by examining what theory and research have told us about personality change in adulthood. Many theorists believe that adult concerns and involvements are patterned in such a way that we can speak about *stages* of adult development. Early (or young) adulthood covers the two decades from 20 to 40, and middle adulthood spans the years from 40 to 60 or 65. These are both discussed in this chapter. Later adulthood (or 'old age') is discussed in Chapter 4.

Erikson's theory

Chapter 1 described Erikson's views on adolescence and his theory that human development occurs through a sequence of psychosocial stages. As far as early and middle adulthood are concerned, Erikson described two primary developmental crises (the sixth and seventh of his psychosocial stages: see Table 1.1, page 9).

The first is the establishment of *intimacy*, which is a criterion of having attained the psychosocial state of adulthood. By intimacy, Erikson means the ability to form close, meaningful relationships with others without 'the fear of losing oneself in the process' (Elkind, 1970). Erikson believed that a prerequisite for intimacy was the attainment of *identity* (the reconciliation of all our various roles into one enduring and stable personality: see page 8). Identity is necessary because we cannot know what it means to love someone and seek to share our life with them until we know who we are and what we want to do with our lives. Thus, genuine intimacy requires us to give up some of our sense of separateness, and we must each have a firm identity to do this.

Intimacy need not involve sexuality. Since intimacy refers to the essential ability to relate our deepest hopes and fears to another person, and in turn to accept another's need for intimacy, it describes the relationship between friends just as much as that between sexual partners (Dacey, 1982). By sharing ourselves with others, our personal identities become fully realised and consolidated. Erikson believed that if a sense of identity were not established with friends or a partner, then *isolation* (a sense of being alone without anyone to share with or care for) would result. We normally achieve intimacy in *young adulthood* (our 20s and 30s), after which we enter *middle age* (our 40s and 50s). This involves the attainment of *generativity*, the second developmental crisis.

Box 2.1 *Generativity*

The central task of the middle years of adulthood is to determine life's purpose or goal, and to focus on achieving aims and contributing to the well-being of others (particularly children). Generativity means being concerned with others beyond the immediate family, such as future generations and the nature of the society and world in which those future generations will live. As well as being displayed by parents, generativity is shown by anyone actively concerned with the welfare of young people and in making the world a better place for them to live and work. People who successfully resolve this developmental crisis establish clear guidelines for their lives and are generally productive and happy within this *directive framework*. Failure to attain generativity leads to *stagnation*, in which people become preoccupied with their personal needs and comforts.

Evaluation of Erikson's theory

The sequence from identity to intimacy may not accurately reflect present-day realities. In recent years, the trend has been for adults to live together before marrying, so they tend to marry later in life than people did in the past (see Chapter 3, page 47). Many people struggle with identity issues (such as career choice) *at the same time* as dealing with intimacy issues.

Additionally, some evidence suggests that females achieve intimacy *before* 'occupational identity'. The typical life course of women involves passing directly into a stage of intimacy without having achieved personal identity. Sangiuliano (1978) argues that most women submerge their identities into those of their partners, and only in mid-life do they emerge from this and search for separate identities and full independence. Sangiuliano's research appears, however, not to have taken into account the possibility that *social class* interacts with gender. For example, amongst working class men, early marriage is seen as a 'good' life pattern. They see early adulthood as a time for 'settling down', having a family and maintaining a steady job. Middle class men and women, by contrast, see early adulthood as a time for exploration, in which different occupations are tried. Marriage tends to occur after this, and 'settling down' does not usually take place before 30 (Neugarten, 1975).

Hodgson & Fischer (1979) discovered sex differences in the relationship between identity and intimacy. Ninety per cent of female university students rated as identity achievers were also rated as showing intimacy in their relationships. However, 52 per cent of those *not* rated as identity achievers were also rated as showing intimacy. Amongst male students, very few showed intimacy without identity.

Erikson's psychosocial stages were meant to be *universal*, applying to both sexes in all cultures. However, he acknowledged that the sequence of stages is different for a woman, who suspends her identity as she prepares to attract the man who will marry her. Men achieve identity before achieving intimacy with a sexual partner, whereas for women, Erikson's developmental crises appear to be fused. As Gilligan (1982) has observed:

'the female comes to know herself as she is known, through relationships with others'.

Neugarten's (1975) findings indicate that as well as describing developmental patterns separately for gender, it is also necessary to do this for social class. This suggests that it is almost certainly impossible to describe *universal* stages for adults. Moreover, there is evidence of a growing prolongation of adolescence.

Box 2.2 *Perpetual adolescence*

According to Sheehy (1996), whilst childhood is ending earlier, adults are prolonging adolescence into their 30s. Indeed, many people are not acknowledging maturity until they reach 40. Sheehy suggests that:

'Adolescence is now prolonged for the middle classes until the end of their 20s, and for blue-collar men and women until their mid-20s, as more young adults live at home longer. True adulthood does not begin until 30. Most Baby Boomers, born after World War II, do not feel fully 'grown up' until they are in their 40s, and even then they resist'.

Beaumont (1996) argues that we have evolved into a generation of 'Peter Pans', perpetually stuck in adolescence:

'You see them in Hyde Park – 30- and 40-somethings on rollerblades and skateboards, hanging out at Glastonbury or discussing the merits of Oasis versus Blur at dinner parties'.

The fictional models of this 'new generation' are Gary and Tony from the BBC television programme *Men Behaving Badly* (see Figure 2.1, page 25), and Patsie and Eddy from *Absolutely Fabulous*. Real-life examples of 'Peter Pans' include Mick Jagger, Cliff Richard and Richard Branson.

According to Orbach (cited in Beaumont, 1996), one problem created by adults who refuse to grow up is their own parenting. Unable to look up to figures of authority themselves, they feel a sense of loss and look to their own children for emotional sustenance in a curious role reversal.

Figure 2.1 *Gary and Tony, the 'perpetual adolescents' in BBC TV's* Men Behaving Badly

Levinson *et al.*'s *Seasons of a Man's Life*

Perhaps the most systematic study of personality and life changes in adulthood began in 1969, when Levinson *et al.* interviewed 40 men aged 35 to 45 from a variety of occupational backgrounds. Transcripts were made of the five to ten tape-recorded interviews that each participant gave over several months. Levinson *et al.* looked at how adulthood is actually *experienced*.

In *The Seasons of a Man's Life*, Levinson *et al.* (1978) advanced a *life structure theory*, defining life structure as the underlying pattern or design of a person's life at any given time. Life structure allows us to 'see how the self is in the world and how the world is in the self', and evolves through a series of *phases* or *periods* which give overall shape to the course of adult development. Adult development comprises a sequence of *eras* which overlap in the form of *cross-era transitions*. These last about five years, terminating the outgoing era and initiating the incoming one. The four eras are pre-adulthood (age 0–22), early adulthood (17–45), middle adulthood (40–65) and late adulthood (60 onwards).

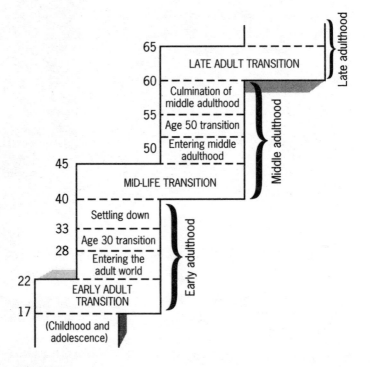

Figure 2.2   *Levinson et al.'s theory of adult development. The life-cycle is divided into four major eras that overlap in the form of cross-era transitions (From Gross, 1996)*

The phases or periods alternate between those that are *stable* (or *structure-building*) and *transitional* (or *structure-changing*). Although each phase involves biological, psychological and social adjustments, family and work roles are seen as central to the life structure at any time, and individual development is interwoven with changes in these roles.

The era of early adulthood

Early adult transition (17–22) is a developmental 'bridge' between adolescence and adulthood.

Box 2.3 *Separation and attachment*

Two key themes of the early adult transition are *separation* and the formation of *attachments* to the adult world. *External* separation involves moving out of the family home, increasing financial independence, and entering more independent and responsible roles and living arrangements. *Internal* separation involves greater psychological distance from the family, less emotional dependence on the parents, and greater differentiation between the self and family. Although we separate from our parents, Levinson *et al.* argue that we never complete the process, which continues throughout life. Attachment involves exploring the world's possibilities, imagining ourselves as part of it, and identifying and establishing changes for living in the world before we become 'full members' of it.

Between ages 22 and 28, we *enter the adult world.* This is the first *structure-building* (rather than *structure-changing*) phase and hence is referred to as the *entry life structure for early adulthood.* In it, we try to fashion:

'a provisional structure that provides a workable link between the valued self and adult society'.

In the *novice phase*, we try to define ourselves as adults and live with the initial choices we make concerning jobs, relationships, lifestyles and values. However, we need to create a balance between 'keeping our options open' (which allows us to explore possibilities without being committed to a given course) and 'putting down roots' (or creating stable life structures).

Our decisions are made in the context of our *dreams* (the 'vague sense' we have of ourselves in the adult world and what we want to do with our lives). We must overcome disappointments and setbacks, and learn to accept and profit from successes, so that the dream's 'thread' does not get lost in the course of 'moving up the ladder' and revising the life structure. To help us in our efforts at self-definition, we look to *mentors*, older and more experienced others, for guidance and direction. Mentors can take a *formal* role in guiding, teaching and helping novices to define their dreams. Alternatively, a mentor's role may be *informal*, providing an advisory and emotionally supportive function (as a parent does).

The *age-30 transition* (28–33) provides an opportunity to work on the flaws and limitations of the first life structure, and to create the basis for a more satisfactory structure that will complete the era of young adulthood. Most of Levinson *et al.*'s participants experienced *age-30 crises* which involved stress, self-doubt, feelings that life was losing its 'provisional quality' and becoming more serious, and time pressure. Thus, the participants saw this as being the time for change, if change was needed. However, for a minority the age-30 transition was crisis-free.

Box 2.4   *Settling down*

The *settling down* (or *culminating life structure for early adulthood*: 33–40) phase represents consolidation of the second life structure. This involves a shift away from tentative choices regarding family and career towards a strong sense of commitment to a personal, familial and occupational future. Paths for success in work and husband and father roles are mapped out and, instead of just beginning to find out what is important and what our opinions are, we see ourselves as responsible adults.

The settling down phase comprises two sub-stages: *early settling down* (33–36) and *becoming one's own man* or *BOOM* (36–40). In the latter, we strive to advance and succeed in building better lives, improve and use our skills, be creative, and in general contribute to society. We want recognition and affirmation from society, but we also want to be self-sufficient and free of social pressure and control. Although a 'boy–man' conflict may be produced, this can represent a step forward. This sub-stage may also see us assume a *mentor role* for someone younger (see above).

The era of middle adulthood

The *mid-life transition* (40–45) involves terminating one life structure, initiating another, and continuing the process of individuation started during the *BOOM* sub-stage. This is a time of soul-searching, questioning and assessing the real meaning of the life structure's achievement. It is sometimes referred to as the *mid-life crisis*, although Levinson *et al.* did not actually use this term. For some people, the change is gradual and fairly painless. For others, however, it is full of uncertainties.

The age-50 mid-life crisis stems from unconscious tensions between attachment and separation, the resurfacing of the need to be creative (which is often repressed in order to achieve a career), and retrospective comparisons between 'dreams' and life's reality.

Most participants in Levinson *et al.*'s study had not reached age 45. Following interviews two years after the study was concluded, some were chosen for more extensive study. However, the evidence for the remaining phases is much less detailed than for the earlier ones.

In entering *middle adulthood* (or *early life structure for middle adulthood*: 45–50), we have resolved (more-or-less satisfactorily) whether what we have committed ourselves to really is worthwhile, and it is again necessary to make choices regarding a new life structure. Sometimes, these choices are defined by *marker events* such as divorce, illness, occupational change, or the death of a loved one. However, the choices may also be influenced by less obvious but significant changes, such as shifts in the enthusiasm for work or in the quality of marriage. As before, the resulting life structure varies in how satisfying it is and how connected it is to the self. It may not be intrinsically happy and fulfilling. The restructuring consists of many steps and there may be setbacks in which options have to be abandoned ('back to the drawing board').

The validity of the 'mid-life crisis'

Just as the 'identity crisis' is part of the popular stereotype of adolescence (see page 8), Levinson *et al.* have helped to make the 'mid-life crisis' part of the common-sense understanding of adult development. Like Erikson, Levinson *et al.* see crisis as *inevitable*. As they note:

'It is not possible to get through middle adulthood without having at least a moderate crisis in either the mid-life transition or the age-50 transition'.

They also see crisis as *necessary*. If we do not engage in soul searching, we will:

'pay the price in a later developmental crisis or in a progressive withering of the self and a life structure minimally connected to the self'.

The view that crisis is both inevitable and necessary (or *normative*, to use Erikson's term) is controversial. People of all ages suffer occasional depression, self-doubt, sexual uncertainty and concerns about the future. Indeed, there appears to be an increasingly wide age range (and a growing number) of people who decide to make radical changes in their life-style, both earlier and later than predicted by Levinson *et al.*'s theory (see Box 2.5).

Durkin (1995) notes that a large proportion of middle-aged people actually feel *more* positive about this phase of life than earlier ones, with only ten per cent reporting feeling as though they had experienced a crisis. For Durkin, the mid-life crisis is not as universal as Levinson *et al.* suggest, and the time and extent to which we experience uncomfortable self-assessments vary as a function of several factors (such as personality). Although the evidence is sparse, going through middle age in a relatively peaceful and untroubled way is actually a *favourable* indicator of future development, that is, a *lack* of emotional disturbance predicts *better* rather than poorer functioning in later life (Rutter & Rutter, 1992).

Figure 2.3 *The image of an older man's attraction to younger women is part of the popular concept of the 'mid-life crisis'. It is portrayed here by Woody Allen and Juliette Lewis in* Husbands and Wives

---

Box 2.5 *'Downshifting'*

According to Tredre (1996), the concept of a mid-life crisis is too narrow in that traditionally, or stereotypically, it refers to someone in his or her late 40s, with grown-up children, who gives up a secure and well-paid 'respectable' career, and moves to a small market town or village in order to enjoy a less stressful, more peaceful and generally better quality of life. We need to spread the net wider nowadays and think in terms of early-, mid- and late-life crises: people of all age groups and walks of life are 'feeling the itch'.

Downshifting refers to voluntarily opting out of a pressurised career and interminably long hours in the office, and often involves giving up an exceptionally well-paid job in a high-profile industry in the pursuit of a more fulfilling way of life. Tredre identifies a number of possible reasons for downshifting, including anti-urbanism (fuelled by concerns over urban pollution), crime, violence, and increasing job insecurity.

Two other components of the mid-life crisis are much less contentious. The first is a wide range of adaptations in the life pattern. Some of these stem from role changes that produce fairly drastic consequences, such as divorce, remarriage, a major occupational change, redundancy or serious illness. Others are more subtle, and include the ageing and likely death of parents, the new role of grandparent, and the sense of loss which sometimes occurs when children have all moved away from the family home (*empty-nest distress*). The impact of some of these life or marker events is discussed in Chapter 3.

The second non-controversial component is the significant change in the *internal* aspects of life structures, which occurs regardless of external events. This involves reappraising achievements and remaining ambitions, especially those to do with work and the relationship with our sexual partner. A fundamental development at this time is the realisation that the final authority for life rests with us. (This relates to Gould's, 1978, 1980, theory: see page 35.) Sheehy (1976) has suggested that men in their 40s begin to explore and develop their more 'feminine' selves (by becoming more nurturant, affiliative and intimate). Women, by contrast, discover their more 'masculine' selves (by becoming more action-oriented, assertive, and ambitious). The passing-by in *opposite directions* produces the pain and distress which is the 'mid-life crisis'.

However, it has been argued that the mid-life crisis is not a stage through which everyone *must* pass. For example, it can stem from several sources, including ineffective adjustment to the normal stresses of growth and transition in middle-age and the reaction of a particularly vulnerable person to these stresses (Hopson & Scally, 1980). The diversity of adult experience makes terms like 'stages' and 'seasons' inappropriate. *Themes*, perhaps, is a better term.

Many stressful biological, social and psychological life changes are likely to occur together in any particular society (Bee & Mitchell, 1980). As a result, most people will experience transitions or crises at roughly the same time in their life-cycles. People will differ regarding how much stress they can tolerate before a 'crisis' is experienced, and in how they respond to it when it does occur. Personal growth may be one response, and changing the major 'external' aspects of our lives (by, for example, changing jobs or, getting divorced) another.

The seasons of a woman's life

Levinson *et al.*'s research was carried out on men, and no women were included in the sample. Similar research investigating women has found similarities with Levinson *et al.*'s findings. However, men and women have been shown to differ in terms of their *dreams*.

Box 2.6 *Women's dreams and 'gender splitting'*

Levinson (1986) argues that a 'gender-splitting' phenomenon occurs in adult development. Men have fairly unified visions of their futures which tend to be focused on their careers. Women, however, have 'dreams' which are more likely to be split between a career and marriage. This was certainly true of academics and business women, although the former were less ambitious and more likely to forego a career, whereas the latter wanted to maintain their careers but at a reduced level. Only the *homemakers* had unified dreams (to be full-time wives and mothers, as their own mothers had been).

Roberts & Newton (1987) saw the family as playing a 'supportive' role for men. Women's dreams were constructed around their relationship with the husband and family, which subordinated their personal needs. So, part of *her* dream is *his* success. For Durkin (1995), this difference in women's and men's priorities may put women at greater risk:

'of disappointment and developmental tension as their investment in others' goals conflict with their personal needs'.

Women who give marriage and motherhood top priority in their 20s tend to develop more individualistic goals for their 30s. However, those who are career-oriented early on in adulthood tend to focus on marriage and family concerns later. Generally, the transitory instability of the early 30s lasts *longer* for women than for men, and 'settling down' is much less clear cut. Trying to integrate career and marriage/family responsibilities is very difficult for most women, who experience greater conflicts than their husbands are likely to.

The validity of stage theories of adult development

Erikson's and Levinson's theories of adult development emphasise a 'ladder-like' progression through an inevitable and universal series of stages. The view that adult development is 'stage-like' has, however, been criticised (Rutter & Rutter, 1992) on the grounds that it underestimates the degree of *individual variability*. Many members of the mainstream working class population do *not* grow or change in systematic ways. Instead, they show many rapid fluctuations, depending on things like relationships, work demands and other life stresses that are taking place (Craig, 1992).

Stage theories also imply a *discontinuity* of development. However, many psychologists maintain there is also considerable *continuity* of personality during adult life. The popular stereotype sees middle adulthood as the time when a person is responsible, settled, contented and at the peak of achievement. People who find that they do not conform to this stereotype tend to blame themselves rather than seeing the stereotype as being wrong (Hopson & Scally, 1980). Schlossberg *et al.* (1978) have suggested that we use some sort of *social clock* to judge whether we are 'on time' with respect to particular life events (such as getting married). If we are 'off time', either early or late, we are *age deviant*. Like other types of deviancy, this can result in social penalties, such as amusement, pity or rejection.

Craig (1992) sees changes in adult thought, behaviour and personality as being less a result of chronological age or specific biological changes, and more a result of personal, social and cultural events or forces. Because of the sheer diversity of experiences in an adult's life, Craig does not believe it is possible to describe major 'milestones' that will apply to nearly everyone.

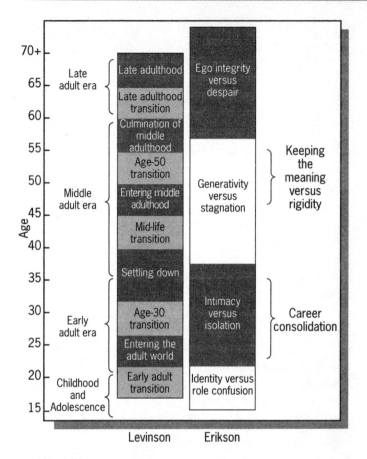

Figure 2.4   *A comparison of Levinson et al.'s and Erikson's adult stages. Note how the former's are defined primarily by age and the latter's by crisis (From Santrock, 1986)*

Gould's theory of the evolution of adult consciousness

Whereas Levinson *et al.* discussed adult development in terms of evolving life structures, Gould (1978, 1980) prefers to talk about the evolution of adult consciousness which occurs when:

'we release ourselves from the constraints and ties of childhood consciousness'.

Gould sees the thrust of adult development as being towards the realisation and acceptance of ourselves as creators of our own lives, and away from the assumption that the rules and standards of childhood determine our destiny. His theory is an extension of the Freudian idea of *separation anxiety*. According to Gould, we have to free ourselves of the *illusion of absolute safety*, an illusion which dominated childhood. This involves *transformations*, giving up the security of the past to form our own ideas. We have to replace the concept of parental dependency with a sense of *autonomy*, or owning ourselves. This, however, is difficult because dependency on parents is a normal feature of childhood. Indeed, without it, childhood would be very difficult. As well as shedding childhood consciousness, Gould believes that our *sense of time* also changes.

Box 2.7 *Our changing sense of time*

Up until age 18 or so, we feel both protected and constrained by our parents, and never quite believe that we will escape the 'family world'. This is like being in a timeless capsule in which 'the future is a fantasy space that may possibly not exist'. However, we begin to glimpse an endless future and see an infinite amount of time ahead of us.

In our 20s, we become confident about being separated from the family. However, we have not yet formed early-adult life structures. Gould (1980) puts it like this:

'Because of all the new decisions and novel experiences that come with setting up new adult enterprises, our time sense, when we're being successful, is one of movement along a chosen path that leads linearly to some obscure prize decades in the future. There is plenty of time, but we're still in a hurry once we've developed a clearer, often stereotyped, picture of where we want to be by then'.

At the end of our 20s, our sense of time incorporates our adult past as well as future. The future is neither infinite nor linear, and we must choose between different options because there isn't time to

---

take them all. From our mid-30s to mid-40s, we develop a sense of urgency that time is running out. We also become aware of our own mortality which, once attained, is never far from our consciousness. How we spend our time becomes a matter of great importance. Additionally, we begin to question whether our 'prize' (freedom from restrictions by those who have formed us – our parents) either exists or, if it does, whether it has been worth it (cf. Levinson *et al.*'s 'dream').

Conclusions

This chapter has considered several theories of personality change in early and middle adulthood. The stage theory approach has been popular, although critics argue that development does not occur in predictable and ordered ways. Whether personality development in adulthood is characterised by stability or change has yet to be resolved.

Summary

- Adulthood is the longest phase of the life-cycle. Early and young adulthood covers the years 20 to 40, whilst middle adulthood spans the years 40 to 60 or 65.

- In Erikson's psychosocial theory, young adulthood involves the establishment of **intimacy**. This can be achieved through friendship as well as through a sexual relationship. Failure to achieve intimacy results in a sense of **isolation**. The central task of middle adulthood is the attainment of **generativity**. Failure to achieve generativity results in **stagnation**.

- The sequence from identity to intimacy may no longer accurately reflect relationship patterns. Many people struggle with issues of identity and intimacy **at the same time**, especially women. Women tend to achieve intimacy **before** 'occupational identity', submerging their identity into their partners'. There are also important social class differences in the timing of marriage and 'settling down'.

- According to Sheehy, whilst childhood is ending earlier, people, especially those from middle class backgrounds, are prolonging adolescence into their 30s.

- Levinson *et al.* were concerned with how adulthood is actually **experienced**. Their **life structure theory** identifies **phases** or **periods** which give overall shape to the course of adult development. These are either **stable (structure-building)** or **transitional (structure-changing)**. A sequence of **eras** overlaps in the form of **cross-era transitions**.

- **Early adult transition** (17–22) is a developmental bridge between adolescence and adulthood. It involves both internal and external **separation** from parents and **attachment** to the adult world.

- **Entry life structure for early adulthood** (22–28) is the first **structure-building** phase. In the novice phase, we make choices in the context of our **dreams**. We look to mentors to help us in the task of self-definition and defining our dreams.

- The **age-30 transition** (28–33) provides an opportunity to create the basis for a more satisfactory life structure that will complete the era of young adulthood. An **age-30 crisis** is commonly experienced.

- The **culminating life structure for early adulthood/settling down** phase (33–40) involves two sub-stages, **early settling down** (33–36) and **becoming one's own man** (BOOM) (36–40), which may involve the assumption of a **mentor role** for some younger adult.

- The **mid-life transition** (40–45) is a time of soul-searching and assessing the meaning of the life-structure achievement (**mid-life crisis**).

- In **early life structure for middle adulthood/entering middle adulthood** (45–50), we must again make choices regarding new life structures. These choices are sometimes defined by **marker events**.

- Levinson *et al.* have helped to make the 'mid-life crisis' part of our common-sense understanding of adult development.

They see crisis as both **inevitable** and **necessary** (**normative**).

- People of all ages suffer crises, and a growing number of people are deciding to make radical changes in their life-style (**downshifting**), both earlier and later than predicted by Levinson *et al.*

- A large proportion of middle-aged people actually feel **more** positive about their lives than earlier, and the mid-life crisis is not as universal as Levinson *et al.* suggest.

- Research involving women has found similarities with Levinson *et al.*'s findings based on their all-male sample. However, there is a 'gender splitting' that occurs in relation to men's and women's **dreams**. Whilst men have fairly unified, career-focused visions of the future, women's dreams are split between career and marriage/family responsibilities.

- The age-30 transition generally lasts longer for women than for men, and 'settling down' is much less clear cut. Trying to integrate career and marriage and family responsibilities is very difficult for most women.

- The view that adult development is 'stage-like' has been criticised on the grounds that it underestimates **individual variability**. Stage theories also imply a **discontinuity of development**, whilst many psychologists stress the **continuity** of adult personality. The sheer diversity of adult experience makes it impossible to describe major 'milestones' that apply to everyone.

- According to Gould, the thrust of adult development is towards the realisation and acceptance of ourselves as creators of our own lives (adult consciousness) and freeing ourselves of the **illusion of absolute safety.**

- Gould also believes that adult development involves a change in the **sense of time.** By the end of our 20s, the future is seen as neither infinite nor linear, and we must make choices. From our mid-30s to mid-40s, we sense that time is running out and are aware of our mortality.

THE IMPACT OF LIFE
EVENTS IN ADULTHOOD

3

Introduction and overview

As Chapter 2 showed (see page 34), evidence concerning the predictability of changes in adult life (or what Levinson, 1986, calls *psychobiosocial transitions*) is conflicting. Three kinds of influence can affect the way we develop in adulthood (Hetherington & Baltes, 1988). *Normative age-graded influences* are biological (such as the menopause) and social (such as marriage and retirement) changes that normally occur at fairly predictable ages. *Normative history-graded influences* are historical events that affect whole generations or cohorts at about the same time (examples include wars, recessions and epidemics). *Non-normative influences* are idiosyncratic transitions such as divorce, unemployment and illness.

Levinson (1986) uses the term *marker events* to refer to the age-graded and non-normative influences. Others prefer the term *critical life events* to describe such influences (although it is perhaps more accurate to describe them as *processes*). Some tend to happen early in adulthood (such as marriage and parenthood). Others occur much later (such as retirement, which marks entry into late adulthood). Yet others (such as bereavement and unemployment) can occur at any age. Studying the impact of events such as these is another way of looking at how we adjust to adulthood. This chapter examines research findings concerning the impact of some of these life events.

Unemployment

Unemployment produces both psychological and physical effects which take time to emerge, rather than occurring immediately after an individual has been made unemployed (Argyle, 1989). One psychological effect is *depression*. As well as being more prevalent amongst the unemployed, depression's severity is strongly correlated with the *length* of unemployment. In the long-term unemployed, a sense of *learned helplessness* (Seligman, 1975) develops, in which they see themselves as being the main cause of their unemployment and believe that nothing can be done to change the state of affairs. Along with other factors associated with unemployment, such as poverty and reduced social support, depression is one that contributes to *suicide*. Suicide is much more common among the unemployed than the employed.

Unemployment is also associated with a *loss of self-esteem* through ceasing to be the bread-winner and becoming a recipient of government benefits. The material hardships of low income bring a financial strain which is greatest when there are dependent children. Not surprisingly, financial problems are themselves a major source of emotional distress.

Box 3.1 *Some major sources of distress among the unemployed*

Length of unemployment: The initial response to unemployment is *shock*, *anger* and *incomprehension*. This is followed by optimism, a feeling of being between jobs (a kind of 'holiday'), coupled with active job searching. As job searching fails, optimism is replaced by *pessimism*, which gives way to *fatalism*. Hopelessness and apathy set in and job hunting is sometimes abandoned completely.

Commitment: Those who are most committed to their jobs are most distressed by unemployment. This might explain why unemployment has a greater negative effect on middle-aged men than young people or married women (Warr, 1987).

Social support: The complex set of relationships enjoyed at work conveys identity and status which are both lost in unemployment. The unemployed typically withdraw from friendships, partly because they cannot afford to pay for drinks, entertainment and so on. Because the unemployed is a group to which most people do not wish to belong, the bonds between the unemployed are weak. Social support, especially from the family, can 'buffer' these effects.

Activity level: Those unemployed who have a structured or organised pattern of life (achieved by unpaid work, pursuing a hobby or

keeping active in other ways) experience less distress than those who adapt by staying in bed, watching a lot of television and 'killing time'. **Perceived cause of unemployment:** During periods of full employment, to be out of work might be seen as a sign of failure. However, because unemployment is widespread and includes people from all sections of society, many unemployed feel less responsible for their plight and more accepting of it. For example, satisfaction with the self is greater among unemployed people when the local level of unemployment is high (Warr, 1984).
(Based on Argyle, 1989)

As well as depression and loss of self-esteem, other mental states associated with unemployment include anxiety, negative affect, self-reported cognitive difficulties, worry about the future, demoralisation and resignation (Dooley & Prause, 1995).

Box 3.2 *Some effects of unemployment*

- Unemployment *causes*, rather than results from, poor psychological health.
- The risk of a person's mental health deteriorating in at least some ways increases compared with an otherwise similar person who does not become unemployed.
- Unemployment puts at risk the mental health of unemployed people and their spouses, children and members of the extended family.
- The implicit assumption that the transition from unemployment to re-employment is symmetrical with that from employment to unemployment is not fully warranted, since some effects of unemployment may persist into the period of re-employment.
- The anticipation of unemployment is at least as distressing as its actual experience.
- Job insecurity is associated with experienced powerlessness and impaired mental health.
- Indicators of psychological stress are associated with measures of both subjective and objective financial stress.
(Based on Fryer, 1992; 1995)

Although unemployment is clearly associated with impaired mental health, Argyle's claim that physical health suffers as a result of unemployment is not as strongly supported. For example, Warr (1984) found that whilst 27 per cent of unemployed men said that their physical health had deteriorated, 11 per cent reported that it had *improved* (due to less work strain and more relaxation and exercise). However, in a ten-year census study of British men who had lost their jobs in 1971, Moser *et al.* (1984) showed that the death rate was 36 per cent higher than for the whole population of males aged between 15 and 64. When social class and age were taken into account, the figure was 21 per cent. The data also indicated that unemployed men's wives were 20 per cent more likely to die prematurely, a risk that was greater in the second half of the decade in which the study was conducted.

Retirement

Unlike unemployment, which is a sudden and generally unanticipated loss of work, retirement is anticipated and many people experience it without undue psychological upheaval (Raphael, 1984). It is, then, both inevitable and often acceptable. However, it may be unacceptable to people when, for example, they see themselves as being 'too young' to stop work.

One consequence of retirement is the loss of everyday, ritualised, patterns of behaviour which contribute to the very fabric of our existence. Whilst the early weeks of retirement may be celebrated, emptiness is experienced for a time following retirement. As the months go by, frustration and a sense of 'uselessness' can set in, and this may produce an angry and irritable response to the world.

Retirement also leads to change. For example, many couples find themselves spending an increased amount of time together. Some people compound the negative aspects of retirement by moving to a new house, which involves loss of familiar surroundings, friendships and neighbourhood networks. The

Figure 3.1   *Victor Meldrew (star of BBC TV's* One Foot in the Grave*) seems to personify the sense of frustration and uselessness that often sets in, especially for men, after the 'honeymoon period' of retirement*

transition from an economically productive to an unproductive role can also be stressful. All of these factors mean that psychological adjustment to retirement is necessary, and those who are able to develop lifestyles that retain continuity with the past, and meet their long-term needs, adjust well.

Retirement is a *process* and *social role* which unfolds through a series of six phases, each of which requires an adjustment to be made (Atchley, 1982, 1985). The phases do not correspond with any particular chronological ages, occur in no fixed order, and not all of them are necessarily experienced by everyone.

Box 3.3 *The six phases in the process of retirement*

1 **Pre-retirement phase:** (i) In the *remote* sub-phase, retirement is seen as being in a reasonably distant future; (ii) the *near* sub-phase may be initiated by the retirement of older friends and colleagues and there may be much anxiety about lifestyle changes, especially financial ones.

2 **Honeymoon phase (immediate post-retirement):** This phase typically involves euphoria, partly due to newfound freedom, and is often a busy period (which may be long or short).

3 **Disenchantment phase:** This involves a slowing down after the honeymoon phase, with feelings of being let down and even depression. The degree of disenchantment is related to declining health and finances. Eagerly anticipated post-retirement activities (e.g. travel) may have lost their original appeal. Disenchantment may be produced by unrealistic pre-retirement fantasies or inadequate preparation for retirement.

4 **Reorientation phase:** This is a time to develop a more realistic view of life alternatives, and may involve exploring new avenues of involvement, sometimes with the help of community groups (e.g. special voluntary or paid jobs for the retired). This helps to decrease feelings of role loss and is a means of achieving *self-actualisation*.

5 **Stability phase:** This involves the establishment of criteria for making choices, allowing people to deal with life in a fairly comfortable and orderly way. They know what is expected of them, what their strengths and weaknesses are, allowing mastery of the retirement role.

6 **Termination phase:** Illness and disability usually make housework and self-care difficult or impossible, leading to the assumption of a sick or disabled (as opposed to retirement) role.

(From Gross, 1996, and based on Atchley, 1982, and Atchley & Robinson, 1982)

People who retire *voluntarily* seem to have little or no difficulty in adjusting. However, those who retire because they have reached a compulsory age tend to be dissatisfied at first, although eventually they adapt. The least satisfied are those whose health is poor when they retire (which may have caused their retirement), although health often improves following retirement.

Bromley (1988) believes that it is the *transition* between employment and retirement that causes adjustment problems. Those who are most satisfied in retirement tend to be scientists, writers and other academics, who simply carry on working with little loss of continuity from very satisfying jobs. Those who discover satisfying leisure activities, with at least some of the characteristics of work, also adjust well.

Some people decide to retire before their job requires them to. This means that retirement cannot be seen as a necessarily sudden and enforced dislocation of a working life, inevitably causing feelings of rejection and leading to physical and psychological ill health. Even after 60 or 65, many people do not actively seek paid work, although the lower level of income in retirement constitutes a strong incentive to work. A woman not only has to adjust to her own retirement, but may also have to adjust to her husband's retirement or to widowhood. However, since home and family still occupy a major part of a working woman's time, she is likely to see retirement as less of a lifestyle change than are men.

Clearly, retirement and unemployment are similar in some respects and different in others. According to Campbell (1981), retirement is an accepted and 'honourable' social status, whereas unemployment is not. Moreover, retirement is seen as a proper reward for a hard life's work, whilst unemployment has the implication of failure, being unwanted, and a 'scrounger' who is 'living on state charity'. Most men might see retirement as a rather benign condition of life, but being unemployed is a disturbing and often degrading experience.

Marriage and divorce

Since over 90 per cent of adults marry at least once, marriage is an example of a normative age-graded influence (see page 40). Marriage is an important transition for many young adults, because it involves a lasting personal commitment to another person, financial responsibilities and, perhaps, family responsibilities. However, it cannot be the *same* type of transition for everyone. In some cultures, for example, people have little choice as to who their partners will be (as is the case in *arranged marriages*).

Marriage and preparation for marriage can be very stressful. Davies (1956) identified mental disorders occurring for the first time in those who were engaged to be married. Typically, these were anxiety and depression, which usually began in connection with an event that hinged on the marriage date (such as booking the reception). Since the disorders improved when the engagement was broken off or the marriage took place, Davies concluded that it was the *decision* to make the commitment that was important, rather than the act of getting married itself.

Box 3.4 *Cohabitation*

Apparently, couples who live together (or *cohabit*) before marriage are actually *more* likely to divorce later, and be *less* satisfied with their marriages, than those who marry without having cohabited. Also, about 40 per cent of couples who cohabit do not marry. Whilst this suggests that cohabitation may prevent some divorces, cohabitees who do marry are more likely to divorce. Bee (1994) argues that this is because people who choose to cohabit are *different* from those who choose not to. As a group, cohabitees seem to be more willing to flout tradition in many ways (such as being less religious and disagreeing that one should stay with a marriage partner no matter what). Those who do not cohabit include a large proportion of 'more traditional' people.

It has long been recognised that mortality is affected by marital status. Married people tend to live longer than unmarried people, are happier, healthier and have lower rates of various mental disorders than the single, widowed or divorced. The excessive mortality of the unmarried relative to the married has generally been increasing over the past two to three decades, and it seems that divorced (and widowed) people in their 20s and 30s have particularly high risks of dying compared with married people of the same age (Cramer, 1995). Measures of marital adjustment indicate that agreement between partners on various issues (a measure of marital compatibility) is positively correlated with other components of relationship adjustment, such as satisfaction, affection and doing various activities together (Eysenck & Wakefield, 1981).

Bee (1994) has argued that the greatest beneficiaries of marriage are men, partly because they are less likely than women to have close confidants outside marriage, and partly because wives provide more emotional warmth and support for husbands than husbands do for wives. Marriage is less obviously psychologically protective for women, not because a confiding and harmonious relationship is any less important for them (indeed, if anything it is more important), but because (a) many marriages do not provide such a relationship and (b) other consequences of marriage differ between the sexes. Although our attitudes towards education and women's careers have changed, Rutter & Rutter (1992), echoing the idea of 'gender-splitting' (see Chapter 2, page 33), have proposed that:

'the potential benefits of a harmonious relationship may, for a woman, be counterbalanced by the stresses involved in giving up a job or in being handicapped in a career progression or promotion through having to combine a career and parenthood'.

According to Turnbull (1995), divorce rates are highest during the first five years of marriage and then peak again after couples have been married for 15–25 years. Divorce is a stressor for both men and women, since it involves the loss of one's major attachment figure and source of emotional support. However, men appear to experience more stress than women. Also, divorce can have serious effects on the psychological adjustment of children whose parents are separating (Richards, 1995).

According to Woollett & Fuller (cited in Cooper, 1996), mothers who have been through a divorce often report experiencing a sense of achievement in their day-to-day activities and a feeling of 'a job well done'. This is because they use their experiences of divorce in a positive way to 'galvanise' them into taking charge of their lives. According to Woollett:

> 'when the marriage breaks down, the mother is thrown into all sorts of things that are unfamiliar. There are new areas, new decisions, and she is forced to cope'.

However, Lewis (cited in Cooper, 1996) argues that:

> 'we must be careful about thinking about the positive changes [divorced women report] because we are always comparing a positive change against the negative feeling that went before. The positive is only relative'.

Parenthood

For most people, parenthood and child-rearing represent key transitions. According to Bee (1994), 90 per cent of adults will become parents, mostly in their 20s and 30s. Parenthood, however, varies in meaning and impact more than any other life transition. It may occur at any time from adolescence to middle age, and for some men, may even occur in late adulthood! Parenthood may also be planned or unplanned, wanted or unwanted, and there are many motives for having children.

Box 3.5 *The variety of parenthood*

Traditionally, parenthood is the domain of the married couple. However, it may involve a single woman, a homosexual couple, a cohabiting couple or couples who adopt or foster children. Since the 1950s, there has been a greater acceptability of sexuality among young people, and this has been accompanied by a marked rise in the number of teenage pregnancies. Equally, though, the increasing importance of work careers for women has also led to more and more couples *postponing* starting a family so that the woman can become better established in her career (see Chapter 2, page 33). As a result of this, there is a new class of middle-aged parents with young children (Turnbull, 1995).

Parenthood brings with it several psychological adaptations. For example, many women worry that their babies may be abnormal, and about the changes in their bodies and how they will cope with parenthood. Another concern is how the relationship with the husband or partner will be affected. Certainly, pregnancy brings many couples closer together, but most men take longer than women to become emotionally involved in the pregnancy, and some men feel left out. This feeling of exclusion may continue after the baby is born, as the mother becomes preoccupied with it.

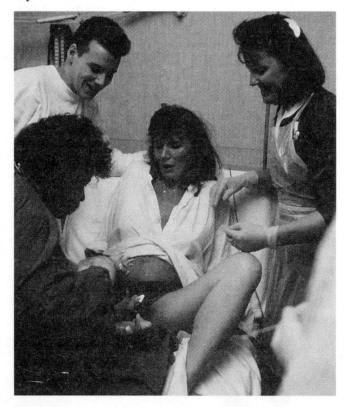

Figure 3.2 *Being at the birth of his child can help to counteract a father's feelings of being excluded during the pregnancy – and afterwards. It can also help him to form an emotional bond with the baby*

Marital satisfaction tends to be highest before children arrive. It then drops and remains relatively low as long as there are dependent children in the home. Finally, it rises again during the 'post-parental' and retirement stages. For new parents, the roles of parent and spouse are at least partially incompatible. New parents report having less time for each other, whether it be conversing, having sex, being affectionate or carrying out routine chores that used to be done together (Bee, 1994).

Parents are, of course, attachment figures for their dependent children. Unlike the relationship with a partner, the relationship with a child is *asymmetrical*. This new form of responsibility can be very stressful and has implications for how parents adapt to these new role demands and the quality of their interactions with the child (Durkin, 1995). Unhappy couples sometimes stay together not 'just for the kids' sake', but because the parental role has sufficient meaning and value for each partner to outweigh the dissatisfaction with their marriage (Levinson *et al.*, 1978).

Regarding *empty-nest distress* (see Chapter 2, page 32), most parents do not find their children's departure from home a distressing time (Durkin, 1995). Indeed, many report that the end of child-rearing responsibilities is a 'liberating experience', and they welcome new opportunities for a closer relationship with their partner, personal fulfilment through work, a return to education and so on. The extent to which women report empty-nest distress may be cohort-related, that is, it may be more typical of women who reached maturity during historical periods when traditional roles were stressed (Durkin, 1995). The *crowded nest* (Datan *et al.*, 1987) can, however, be a source of stress. This occurs when grown-up children opt *not* to leave home, which defies the demands of the 'social clock' established by preceding generations. Parents find it difficult to adjust to 'adult children' living at home, especially if the parents themselves are still doing much of the material providing.

Bereavement

The older we become, the more likely it is that we will suffer the loss, through death, of loved ones, parents, husbands or wives, siblings, friends and even our children. We refer to such losses as *bereavement*. The psychological and bodily reactions that occur in people who suffer bereavement are called grief. The 'observable expression of grief' (Parkes & Weiss, 1983) is called *mourning*, although mourning is often used to refer to the social conventions surrounding death such as funerals, and wearing dark clothes.

Box 3.6 *The three phases of 'griefwork'*

Engel (1962) sees *griefwork* (the process of mourning through which a bereaved person adjusts to a loss) as comprising three stages or phases.

- **Disbelief and shock:** This can last for a few days and involves the refusal to accept the truth of what has happened.
- **Developing awareness:** This is the gradual realisation and acknowledgement of what has happened. It is often accompanied by feelings of guilt, apathy, exhaustion and anger.
- **Resolution:** The bereaved individual views the situation realistically, begins to cope without the deceased, establishes a new identity and comes to accept fully what has happened. This phase marks the completion of 'griefwork'.

(Based on Engel, 1962)

Although researchers differ over the details of the stages or phases of the grieving process, it is widely agreed that grief follows some sort of natural progression which must be experienced if healthy adjustment to the loss is to be achieved. However, instead of stages or phases, some researchers prefer to talk about the *components* of grief. Ramsay & de Groot (1977), for example, have identified nine components, some of which occur early and some late in the grieving process.

Box 3.7 *Ramsay and de Groot's nine components of grief*

1 **Shock:** Usually the first response, most often described as a feeling of 'numbness', which can also include pain, calm, apathy, depersonalisation and derealisation. It is as if the feelings are so strong that they are 'turned off'. This can last from a few seconds to several weeks.
2 **Disorganisation:** The inability to do the simplest thing or, alternatively, organising the entire funeral and then collapsing.
3 **Denial:** Behaving as if the deceased were still alive, a defence against feeling too much pain. It is usually an early feature of grief but one that can recur at any time. A common form of denial is searching behaviour (e.g. waiting for the deceased to come home, or having hallucinations of them).
4 **Depression:** Emerges as the denial breaks down but can occur, usually less frequently and intensely, at any point during the grieving process. It can consist of either 'desolate pining' (a yearning and longing, an emptiness 'interspersed with waves of intense psychic pain') or 'despair' (feelings of helplessness, the blackness of the realisation of powerlessness to bring back the dead).
5 **Guilt:** Can be both real and imagined, for actual neglect of the deceased when they were alive, or for angry thoughts and feelings.
6 **Anxiety:** Can involve fear of losing control of one's feelings, of going mad or more general apprehension about the future (changed roles, increased responsibilities, financial worries, and so on).
7 **Aggression:** Can take the form of irritability towards family and friends, outbursts of anger towards God or fate, doctors and nurses, the clergy or even the person who has died.
8 **Resolution:** An emerging acceptance of the death, a 'taking leave of the dead and acceptance that life must go on'.
9 **Reintegration:** Putting acceptance into practice by reorganising one's life in which the deceased has no place. However, pining and despair may reappear on anniversaries, birthdays, and so on.

(Based on Gross, 1996)

Whether everyone experiences all the components identified by Ramsay and de Groot is questionable, and there are wide individual differences in grieving patterns. Grief is not a simple, universal process through which we all go (Stroebe *et al.*, 1993).

Normal and abnormal grieving

Distinguishing normal from pathological grief is difficult. Parkes & Weiss (1983) identify prolonged, incapacitating grief (*chronic* grief) as the most common variant of the usual pattern of grieving. Hinton (1975) identifies three other abnormal patterns. The first is an exaggeration of the *numbness* associated with the shock of the loss. The second is the 'shading' of some of the more immediate responses into *neurotic forms of emotional distress*. These include fears of being alone, enclosed spaces, of one's own death, and feelings of depersonalisation (a sense of being unreal or unfamiliar to oneself). The third pattern is the appearance of *physical symptoms*. Sometimes these accompany, and sometimes overshadow, the emotional disturbance. Such symptoms include fatigue, insomnia, loss of appetite and weight, headaches and palpitations.

According to Stroebe *et al.* (1993), both widows and widowers have a greater risk of suffering illness and dying following the death of a spouse than married people of a similar age. Parkes *et al.* (1969) see this risk as being largely confined to the first six months after the bereavement and identify *self-neglect*, *suicide* and *cardiac disease* (a 'broken heart') as the important factors. In widowers, death sometimes occurs through a disease similar to that experienced by the wife.

Box 3.8   *Recovery from bereavement or adaptation to it?*

Lieberman (1993) has criticised traditional bereavement research for its underlying assumption that bereavement is a stressor that upsets a person's equilibrium and requires a return to a normal and balanced state. Recovery is not a simple 'return to baseline' level of

> functioning (Weiss, 1993). Both Lieberman and Weiss see 'adaptation' to bereavement as being a better term than 'recovery' from bereavement. Whilst the majority of bereaved people stop grieving intensely after a year or two, a minority continue to do so for longer, and aspects of grief may never end for some otherwise normally adjusted and bereaved individuals. For Stroebe *et al.* (1993):
> 'if there has been a strong attachment to a lost loved one, emotional involvement is likely to continue, even for a lifetime'.
> Adjustment is more difficult when a death is 'off time', as is the case in sudden accidents (Lopata, 1988).

Coming to terms with death

Most adolescents and young adults rarely think about their own deaths, since death is an event far removed in time. Some people even engage in an *illusion of immortality*, and completely avoid confronting the fact that their own days are numbered (Barrow & Smith, 1979). As people age, however, so their thoughts become increasingly preoccupied with death. Our attitude towards death is ambivalent: sometimes we shut it out and deny it, and sometimes we desperately want to talk about it and share our fears of the unknown. Kübler-Ross (1969) uses the term *anticipatory grief* to describe how the terminally ill come to terms with their own imminent death. One common feature of this is *reminiscing*. This may be a valuable way of 'sorting out' the past and present (Butler, 1963). The recognition of impending death allows us to re-examine old conflicts, consider how we have treated others, and come to some conclusion about our lives. This *life review* may result in a new sense of accomplishment, satisfaction and peace (and corresponds to Erikson's *ego-integrity*: see Chapter 4, page 74).

Coming to terms with our own deaths is a crucial *task* of life which Peck (1968) calls *ego-transcendence* versus *ego-preoccupation*. We may review our lives privately (or internally), or we may share our memories and reflections with others. By helping us to organise a final perspective on our lives for ourselves, and leaving records that will live on with others after we have died, sharing serves a double purpose.

Figure 3.3 *Looking through old photographs represents a form of reminiscing, part of the life review in which the elderly person tries to come to terms with his/her death*

Conclusions

Several critical life (or marker) events or processes have been identified. These include unemployment, retirement, marriage, divorce, parenthood and bereavement. Psychological research has told us much about their effects and how they help us understand adjustment to adulthood.

Summary

- Whilst marriage and parenting, and retirement, tend to occur in early and late adulthood respectively (**normative**, **age-graded influences**), bereavement and unemployment can occur at any age (**non-normative influences**). These are also called **marker events** or **critical life events**.

- **Unemployment** produces both physical and psychological effects, including depression. The long-term unemployed seem to develop a sense of **learned helplessness**. This contributes to **suicide**, which is far more common among the unemployed.

- Unemployment is also associated with a **loss of self-esteem**. Distress is increased amongst those most committed to their jobs, who lack social support, whose level of activity is low and who perceive the cause of unemployment as personal incompetence.

- Unemployment can cause anxiety, negative affect, self-reported cognitive difficulties, worry about the future, demoralisation, resignation and powerlessness. Evidence regarding physical health is more mixed than that for mental health.

- **Retirement** is an inevitable, often acceptable, anticipated loss of work. It is a **process** and **social role** which proceeds through six phases, each requiring a different adjustment.

- People who retire **voluntarily** have little or no difficulty in adjusting, compared with those who retire because they have reached retirement age or whose health is poor. It is the **transition** between employment and retirement that causes adjustment problems.

- **Married people** tend to live longer, and are happier, healthier and have lower rates of mental disorder than unmarried people. Men benefit most from marriage, partly because they are less likely than women to have close confidants outside marriage, and partly because wives provide more emotional warmth and support for their husbands than vice versa. The potential benefits of marriage for women may be counterbalanced by the stresses involved in having to combine parenthood with a career.

- Couples who **cohabit** before marriage are more likely to divorce later or be dissatisfied with their marriages than those who don't cohabit.

- **Parenthood** has greater variability in meaning and impact than any other life transition. Whilst pregnancy can bring couples closer together, men can feel excluded, especially after their babies are born, thus pulling the parents further apart.

- Marital satisfaction tends to peak before children arrive, then drops and remains relatively low until the 'post-parental' and retirement stages, when it rises again. There is little support for **empty-nest distress**. The **crowded nest** is likely to be more stressful.

- As we grow older, we are more likely to suffer **bereavement**. Griefwork comprises three stages: disbelief and shock, developing awareness, and resolution. Ramsay and de Groot prefer to talk about the **components** of grief, which do not occur in a fixed order and which are not necessarily experienced by everyone. There are wide individual differences in grieving patterns.

- Perhaps the commonest form of pathological grief is **chronic grief**. Others include an exaggeration of the **numbness** associated with the shock of the loss, **neurotic forms of emotional distress** and **physical symptoms**. Both widows and widowers are more likely to suffer illness and die compared with married people of a similar age.

- A common feature of **anticipatory grief** is reminiscing, a valuable way of sorting out our lives and relationships. This **life review** may produce a new sense of achievement, satisfaction and peace (corresponding to Erikson's **ego-integrity**).

ADJUSTMENT TO LATE ADULTHOOD

4

Introduction and overview

'Growing up' is normally taken to be something desirable and almost an end in itself. By contrast, 'growing old' has traditionally had negative connotations. The negative view of ageing is based on the *decrement model*, which sees ageing as a process of decay or decline in physical and mental health, intellectual abilities and social relationships.

An alternative to the decrement model is the *personal growth model*, which stresses the potential advantages of late adulthood or 'old age', and this much more positive attitude is how ageing has been studied within the lifespan approach. Kalish (1982), for example, emphasises the increase in leisure time, the reduction in many day-to-day responsibilities, and the ability to pay attention only to matters of high priority among the elderly. Older people respond to the reality of a limited and finite future by ignoring many of life's inconsequential details, and instead channel their energies into what is really important.

This chapter considers some of the theories and research concerned with the adjustment to late adulthood or old age. It begins by looking at what is meant by the term 'old' and at some of the physical and psychological changes that occur in late adulthood.

The meaning of 'old'

People today are living longer and retaining their health better than any previous generation (Baltes & Baltes, 1993). The proportion of older people in the British population has increased dramatically in recent years. In 1961, two per cent of the population (one million people) were aged 80 or over. In 1991, this figure had risen to four per cent (2.2 million). The number of centenarians has risen from 271 (in 1951), to 1185 (1971), to 4400 (1991). In 1997, the number stood at 8000 with projections of 12,000 (2001) and 30,000 (2030) (McCrystal, 1997). Because of this *demographic imperative* (Swensen, 1983), developmental psychologists have become increasingly interested in our older years. But what do we mean by 'old'? Kastenbaum's (1979) 'The ages of me' questionnaire assesses how people see themselves at the present moment in relation to their age.

Box 4.1   *Kastenbaum's 'Ages of me' questionnaire*

- My *chronological* age is my actual or official age, dated from my time of birth. My chronological age is ...
- My *biological* age refers to the state of my face and body. In other people's eyes, I *look* as though I am about ... years of age. In my own eyes, I judge my body to be like that of a person of about ... years of age.
- My *subjective* age is indicated by how I feel. Deep down inside, I really feel like a person of about ... years of age.
- My *functional* age, which is closely related to my social age, refers to the kind of life I lead, what I am able to do, the status I believe I have, whether I work, have dependent children and live in my own home. My thoughts and interests are like those of a person of about ... years of age, and my position in society is like that of a person of about ... years of age.

(Adapted from Kastenbaum, 1979)

Figure 4.1   *Whilst (c) might depict someone's chronological age, (a) might correspond to his biological age and (b) might represent his subjective age*

Few people, irrespective of their chronological age, describe themselves *consistently*. Thus, we often give different responses to the ages identified by Kastenbaum. For example, people in their 20s and above usually describe themselves as feeling younger than their chronological ages, and this is also true for many people in their 70s and 80s. People also prefer to 'be younger', that is, we generally consider ourselves to be *too* old. Very few people over 20 say they want to be older.

It seems, then, that knowing a person's chronological age isn't particularly helpful in allowing us to say anything meaningful about the sort of life that person leads. However, one of the dangerous aspects of *ageism* is that chronological age is assumed to be an accurate indicator of all the other ages. We tend to infer that people over 60 have certain characteristics which, taken together, make up the decrement model (illustrated by expressions like 'past it' and 'over the hill'). Stereotypes of the elderly are more deeply entrenched than (mis)conceptions of gender differences. It is therefore not surprising that people are overwhelmingly unenthusiastic about becoming 'old' (Stuart-Hamilton, 1997). By recognising the different 'ages of me', the idea of ageing as decay should be dispelled and lead to a more analytical and positive approach to old age (cf. Kalish, 1982).

Box 4.2 *A decade-by-decade description of 'the elderly'*

The young old (60–69): This period marks a major transition. Most adults must adapt to new role structures in an effort to cope with the losses and gains of the decade. Income is reduced due to retirement. Friends and colleagues start to disappear. Although physical strength wanes somewhat, a great many 'young old' have surplus energy and seek out new and different activities.

The middle-aged old (70–79): This is often marked by loss or illness. Friends and family may die. The middle-aged old must also cope with reduced participation in formal organisations, which can lead to restlessness and irritability. Their own health problems become more severe. The major developmental task is to maintain the personality re-integration achieved in the previous decade.

> **The old old (80–89):** The old old show increased difficulty in adapting to and interacting with their surroundings. They need help in maintaining social and cultural contacts.
> **The very old old (90–99):** Although health problems become more acute, the very old old can successfully alter their activities to make the most of what they have. The major advantage of old age is freedom from responsibilities. If previous crises have been resolved satisfactorily, this decade may be joyful, serene and fulfilling.
> (Based on Burnside *et al.*, 1979, and Craig, 1992)

The aged are not one cohesive group (Craig, 1992). Rather, they are a collection of sub-groups, each of which has unique problems and capabilities, but all of whom share to some degree the age-related difficulties of reduced income, failing health and the loss of loved ones. For Craig, however:

'having a problem is not the same as being a problem, and the all-too-popular view of those over age 65 as needy, non-productive, and unhappy needs revision'.

Similarly, Dietch (1995) has commented that:

'life's final stage is surrounded by more myths, stereotypes and mis-information than any other developmental phase'.

Exactly why there is an upper limit for how long humans can live is not known. According to *genetic clock* or *programmed theory*, ageing is built into every organism through a genetic code that informs cells when to stop working. This is supported by the finding that rare human conditions involving accelerated ageing are the result of defective genes, and also by the observation that identical twins have very similar life-spans. *Accumulated damages theory*, by contrast, sees ageing as a consequence of damage resulting from the wear-and-tear of living. Like a machine, a body eventually wears out as a result of accumulated damage from continued, non-stop use. As we grow older, our cells lose the ability to replace or repair damaged components and eventually cease to function.

Physical and psychological changes in old age

Physical changes

Bee & Mitchell (1980) have summarised the major physical changes that occur in old age.

Box 4.3 *Physical changes in old age*

Smaller: Connective tissues holding the long bones together become compressed and flattened. As a result, height tends to decrease. Changes in calcium metabolism lead to a smaller total body weight than in younger people. Muscle mass is reduced, and some organs (e.g. the bladder) get smaller.

Slower: Since nerve impulses travel more slowly to and from the brain, reaction time is slower. Older people recover more slowly under stressful conditions since the immune system functions less effectively. Fractures take longer to heal, and the renewal of liver and skin cells also slows down.

Weaker: Because of gradual changes in calcium metabolism, bones become brittle and break more easily. Muscles also become weaker. In general, the senses become less efficient.

Lesser: The gradual lessening of elastic tissue in the skin causes wrinkling and sagging. The ear drum and lens of the eye lose some elasticity, producing problems in hearing and seeing. Blood vessels also become less elastic which can give rise to circulatory problems.

Fewer: Body hair becomes more sparse, and the number of teeth and taste buds is reduced (hence food does not taste as good to older people).

(Adapted from Bee & Mitchell, 1980)

Many of the declines that occur in old age can be compensated for. Moreover, regular exercise can significantly reduce the deterioration of many bodily functions, since tissue *disuse* accounts for about half the functional decline between the ages of 30 and 70.

Psychological changes

It is commonly believed that old age is associated with a decrease in cognitive abilities. Until recently, it was thought that intellectual capacity peaked in the late-teens or early 20s, levelled off, and then began to decline fairly steadily during middle age and more rapidly in old age. The evidence on which this claim was based came from *cross-sectional studies* (studying *different* age groups at the same time). However, we cannot draw firm conclusions from such studies, because the age groups compared represent different cohorts who have had different *experiences* (the *cohort effect*). Unless we know how 60-year-olds, say, performed when they were 40 and 20, it is impossible to say whether or not intelligence declines with age.

An alternative methodology is the *longitudinal study* (the *same* people are tested and re-tested at *various* times during their lives). Several studies have produced data contradicting the results of cross-sectional studies, indicating that at least some people retain their intellect well into middle age and beyond (Holahan & Sears, 1995). However, the evidence suggests that there are some age-related changes in different *kinds* of intelligence and *aspects* of memory.

Changes in intelligence

Although psychologists have always disagreed about the definition of intelligence, there is general acceptance that it is *multi-dimensional* (composed of a number of different abilities). *Crystallised intelligence* results from accumulated knowledge, including a knowledge of how to reason, language skills and an understanding of technology. This type of intelligence is linked to education, experience and cultural background, and is measured by tests of general information. *Fluid intelligence* refers to the ability to solve novel and unusual problems (those not previously encountered). It allows us to perceive and draw inferences about relationships among patterns of stimuli and to conceptualise abstract information, which aids problem-solving.

Fluid intelligence is measured by tests using novel and unusual problems not based on specific knowledge or any particular previous learning.

Crystallised intelligence *increases* with age, and people tend to continue improving their performance until near the end of their lives (Horn, 1982). Using the *cross-longitudinal* method (in which different groups of people of different ages are followed up over a long period of time), Schaie & Hertzog (1983) reported that fluid intelligence declines for all age groups over time, having peaked between the ages of 20 and 30. The decline of fluid intelligence with age, but the relative constancy (and improvement) of crystallised intelligence is difficult to explain. The tendency to continue to add to our knowledge as we grow older could account for the constancy of crystallised intelligence. The decline in fluid intelligence may be an inevitable part of the ageing process related to the reduced efficiency of neurological functioning. Alternatively, we might be more likely to maintain our crystallised abilities because we exercise them on a regular basis (Denney & Palmer, 1981). In old age, however, we may be less frequently challenged to use our fluid abilities (Cavanaugh, 1995).

Changes in memory

Some aspects of memory appear to decline with age, possibly because we become less effective at processing information (which may underlie cognitive changes in general: Stuart-Hamilton, 1994). On recall tests, older adults *generally* perform more poorly than younger adults. However, the reverse is sometimes true, as shown by Maylor's (1994) study of the performance of older contestants' performance on *Mastermind*. On recognition tests, the differences between younger and older people are less apparent and may even disappear. As far as *everyday memory* is concerned, the evidence indicates that the elderly do have trouble recalling events from their youth and early life (Miller & Morris, 1993).

Figure 4.2 *Former Conservative Prime Ministers, Margaret Thatcher and Edward Heath, are well known for their political disagreements. If recent reports on ageing are to be believed, Thatcher will have difficulty remembering them, whilst Heath will remember them with irritation*

Significant memory deficits are one feature of *dementia*, the most common form of which is *Alzheimer's disease*. However, over 90 per cent of people above 65 show *little* deterioration (Diamond, 1978). The loss of cortical neurons is minimal in most humans until very late in life, and even in old age such neurons seem capable of responding to enriched conditions by forming additional functional connections with other neurons. Support for this comes from Rogers *et al.*'s (1990) finding that those who keep mentally active are those who maintain their cognitive abilities. The view that decline is wired into the nervous system has also been challenged by those who believe that *negative cultural stereotypes* of ageing actually *cause* memory decline in the elderly.

Box 4.4 *The influence of stereotypes on memory*

Levy & Langer (1994) investigated the memory capabilities of hearing Americans, members of the American deaf community and people from mainland China. It was assumed that members of the deaf community were less likely to have been exposed to negative cultural stereotypes. People from mainland China were chosen because of the high esteem in which Chinese society holds its aged members. The older American deaf participants and the Chinese participants performed much better on memory tasks than the older American hearing participants.

Also, younger hearing Americans held less positive views of ageing than any of the other groups. Amongst the older participants, attitudes towards ageing and memory performance were positively correlated. Levy and Langer believe that negative stereotypes about ageing may become *self-fulfilling prophecies,* in which low expectations mean that people are less likely to engage in activities that will help them maintain their memory abilities.

The subliminal (below conscious awareness) presentation of negative self-stereotypes (e.g. 'Because of my age I am forgetful') tended to worsen memory performance, whilst positive self-stereotypes (e.g. 'Because of my age I have acquired wisdom) tended to improve it (Levy, 1996). Levy found no such effect with young participants, for whom stereotypes of ageing are less salient.

Social changes in old age

Social disengagement theory

Cumming & Henry (1961) attempted to describe what happens to us socially when we grow old. *Social disengagement theory* was based on a five-year study of 275 50–90-year-olds in Kansas City, USA. Bromley (1988) has defined disengagement as:

'a systematic reduction in certain kinds of social interaction. In its simplest and crudest form, the theory of disengagement states that diminishing psychological and biological capacities of people in later life necessitates a severance of the relationships they have with younger people in the central activities of society, and the replacement of these older individuals by younger people. In this way, society renews itself and the elderly are free to die'.

According to Cumming (1975), social disengagement is the withdrawal of society from the individual (through compulsory retirement, children growing up and leaving home, the death of a spouse and so on) and the withdrawal from society of the individual (through reduced social activities and a more solitary life). Hence, the withdrawal is mutual.

Cumming sees disengagement as having three aspects. *Shrinkage of life space* refers to the fact that as we age, we tend to interact with fewer others, and begin to occupy fewer roles. *Increased individuality* means that in the roles that remain, older people are much less governed by strict rules and expectations. Finally, the healthy, older adult actively disengages from roles and relationships and turns increasingly inward and away from interactions with others, as if preparing for death (*acceptance – even embrace – of these changes*). Withdrawal is seen as the most appropriate and successful way to age.

An evaluation of social disengagement theory

Bee (1994) sees Cumming's first two aspects as being beyond dispute. However, the third is more controversial because of its view of disengagement as a natural and *inevitable* process rather than an imposed one, and because it may not accurately describe and account for what happens. Bromley (1988) has offered three main criticisms of social disengagement theory. First, such a view of ageing encourages a policy of segregation, even indifference, to the elderly, and the very destructive belief that old age has no value (the *practical* criticism). Second, disengagement is not a true theory, but more a *proto-theory* (a collection of loosely related assumptions and arguments: the *theoretical* criticism). The most serious criticism is *empirical* and concerns whether *everyone* actually does disengage.

Box 4.5 *Do the elderly disengage?*

Although retirement brings losses in social relationships (as when children leave home or a spouse dies), relationships with others (in particular grandchildren, neighbours and friends) go some way to replacing them. In later life, the *quality* of activities and relationships may become more important than their *quantity*. As a result, older people are more likely to seek engagement and activity.

Evidence supporting this came from Havighurst *et al.*'s (1968) follow-up of about half the sample originally studied by Cumming & Henry (1961). Although increasing age was accompanied by increasing disengagement, at least some of those studied remained active and engaged. Amongst the active and engaged there were high levels of contentment, and the most active were the happiest. The fact that those who disengage the least are the happiest, have the highest morale and live the longest, contradicts social disengagement theory's view that the tendency to withdraw from mainstream society is natural and an inherent part of the ageing process (Bee, 1994). Whilst some people do choose to lead socially isolated lives and find contentment in them, such disengagement does not appear to be necessary for overall mental health in old age.

Bromley (1988) believes that it is generally more accurate to speak of 'industrial' (rather than 'social') disengagement and increased socio-economic dependence. In this way, the origins and circumstances of retirement are kept in focus. For example, many of the past social conditions forcing adults into restricted environments have changed (Turner & Helms, 1989). Improved health care, earlier retirement age and higher educational levels have opened up new areas of pursuit for the elderly and made more active life-styles possible. In Kermis' (1984) view:

'disengagement represents only one of many possible paths of ageing. It has no blanket application to all people'.

Disengagement may also be *cohort specific*, that is, it may have been adaptive to withdraw from an ageist society in the 1950s, but not in a more enlightened culture. Moreover, an individual rarely disengages from all roles to the same degree. Psychological disengagement may not, therefore, coincide with disengagement from social roles. The disposition to disengage is a *personality dimension* as well as a characteristic of ageing (Bromley, 1988). Havighurst *et al.*'s (1968) follow-up study identified several different personality types. These included *reorganisers*, who were involved in a wide range of activities and reorganised their lives to substitute for lost activities, and the *disengaged*, who voluntarily moved away from role commitments. Consistent with disengagement theory, the disengaged reported low levels of activity but high 'life satisfaction'.

Activity (or re-engagement) theory

The major alternative to disengagement theory is *activity* (or *re-engagement*) *theory* (Havighurst, 1964; Maddox, 1964). Activity theory says that except for inevitable changes in biology and health, older people are the same as middle-aged people, with essentially the same psychological and social needs. Decreased social interaction in old age is the result of the withdrawal by society from the ageing person and happens against the wishes of most elderly people. The withdrawal is *not* mutual.

Optimal ageing involves staying active and managing to resist the 'shrinkage' of the social world. This can be achieved by maintaining the activities of middle age for as long as possible, and then finding substitutes for work or retirement and for spouses and friends upon their death. It is important for older adults to maintain their *role counts* (to ensure they always have several different roles to play).

An evaluation of activity theory

There are many exceptions to the 'rule' that the greater the level of activity, the greater the level of satisfaction. Some elderly people seem satisfied with disengagement (see above). This suggests that activity theory *alone* cannot explain successful ageing. People will select a style of ageing best suited to their personality and past experience or lifestyle, and there is no single way to age successfully (Neugarten & Neugarten, 1987). Some people may develop new interests or pursue in earnest those they did not have time enough for during their working lives. Others will be developing relationships with grandchildren or even great-grandchildren, remarrying or perhaps getting married for the first time. Yet others will go on working part time or in a voluntary capacity in their local community.

Figure 4.3   *The elderly couple above seem to fit the stereotype of the withdrawn, isolated, 'disengaged' person, whilst the couple below illustrate an alternative, but less common, stereotype, of the person who remains as active in old age as when he/she was middle-aged*

As a counterbalance to disengagement theory, activity theory sees the natural tendency of most elderly people as associating with others, particularly in group and community affairs, although this is often blocked by present-day retirement practices. Whilst disengagement enables or obliges older people to relinquish certain roles (namely those they cannot adequately fulfil), activity or re-engagement prevents the consequences of disengagement from going too far in the direction of isolation, apathy and inaction.

An evaluation of theories of ageing

Both disengagement and activity theories refer to a legitimate process through which some people come to terms with the many changes that accompany ageing (they are *options*: Hayslip & Panek, 1989). Just as disengagement may be involuntary (as in the case of poor health), so we may face involuntarily high levels of activity (as in looking after grandchildren). Both disengagement and activity may, therefore, be equally maladaptive. Quite possibly, disengagement theory actually *under*estimates, and activity theory *over*estimates, the degree of control people have over the 'reconstruction' of their lives. Additionally, both theories see ageing as essentially the same for all people. For Turner & Helms (1989), however:

'personality is the pivotal factor in determining whether an individual will age successfully, and activity and disengagement theories alone are inadequate to explain successful ageing'.

Increasingly, theorists see development as a lifespan phenomenon, and therefore adjustments to old age or late adulthood are an extension of personality styles (Baltes, 1987). Theoretical emphasis is therefore placed on the *continuity* between earlier and later phases of life. Satisfaction, morale and adaptations in later life generally appear to be closely related to a person's lifelong personality style and general way of dealing with stress and change (Reedy, 1983). As Reedy notes:

'In this sense, the past is the prologue to the future. While the personality changes somewhat in response to various life events and changes, it generally remains stable throughout all of adult life'.

Social exchange theory

Activity theory oversimplifies the issues involved in adjusting to late adulthood and has received little empirical support. As has been seen, activity can decline without seriously affecting morale. Indeed, a more leisurely lifestyle, with fewer responsibilities, can be regarded as one of the *rewards* of old age. This view is at the centre of *social exchange theory*. According to Dyson (1980), both disengagement and activity theories fail to take sufficient account of the physical and economic factors which might limit people's choices about how they age. Rather than accounting for how most people do age, both theories tell us what the elderly *should* be doing and are therefore *prescriptive*. Disengagement and activity theories also involve *value judgements* about what it is to age successfully (Hayslip & Panek, 1989).

For Dyson, a more useful approach is to see the process of adjusting to ageing in general, and retirement in particular, as a sort of *contract* between the individual and society. We give up our roles as economically active members of society when we retire, but in *exchange* we receive increased leisure time, take on fewer responsibilities and so on (Dowd, 1975). Although the contract is largely unwritten and not enforceable, most people will probably conform to the expectations about being elderly which are built into social institutions and stereotypes.

Psychosocial theory

Another alternative to disengagement and activity theories is Erikson's *psychosocial theory* (see Chapter 2). A more valid and useful way of looking at what all elderly people have in common might be to examine the importance of old age as a stage of development, albeit the last (which is where its importance lies). This brings us back to the personal growth model (see page 59), which stresses the advantages and positive aspects of ageing.

In old age, there is a conflict between *ego-integrity* (the positive force) and *despair* (the negative force). The task is to end this stage, and hence life, with greater ego-integrity than despair. This achievement represents successful ageing. However, as with the other psychosocial stages, we cannot avoid the conflict which occurs as a result of inevitable biological, psychological and social forces. For Erikson, the important thing is how successfully this is resolved. Therefore, the task of ageing is to take stock of one's life, to look back over it, and assess and evaluate how worthwhile and fulfilling it has been.

Box 4.6 *The characteristics of ego-integrity*

- Life does have a purpose and makes sense.
- Within the context of our lives as a whole, what happened was somehow inevitable and could only have happened when and how it did.
- A belief that all of life's experiences offer something of value. We can learn from everything that happens to us. Looking back, we can see how we have grown psychologically as a result of life's ups and downs, triumphs and failures, calms and crises.
- Seeing our parents in a new light and being able to understand them better because we have lived through our own adulthood and have probably raised children of our own.
- Seeing that what we share with other humans, past, present and future, is the inevitable cycle of birth and death. Whatever the differences (be they historic, cultural, economic and so on), all of us have this much in common. In the light of this, death 'loses its sting'.

Lack or loss of ego-integrity is signified by a fear of death, which is the most conspicuous symptom of despair. In despair, we express the feeling that it is too late to undo the past and put the clock back in order to right wrongs or do what hasn't been done. Life is not a 'rehearsal' and this is the only chance we get.

Conclusions

Several theories concerned with adjustment to late adulthood have been advanced. Of these, social disengagement theory and activity (or re-engagement) theory have attracted a great deal of research interest. Whilst there is some evidence consistent with both theories, neither is a completely satisfactory account, and several factors not considered by the theories appear to contribute to 'successful ageing'.

Summary

- Whilst 'growing up' has positive connotations, 'growing old' has negative ones, reflecting the **decrement model**. An alternative, more positive view, is the **personal growth model**.
- The proportion of older people in the British population has increased dramatically and is expected to go on increasing. This **demographic imperative** has made developmental psychologists much more interested in late adulthood.
- Age can be defined in different ways, specifically **chronological**, **biological**, **subjective** and **functional** (closely related to **social**). Few people, regardless of chronological age, describe themselves **consistently**.
- Although chronological age tells us little about a person's lifestyle, one feature of **ageism** is the assumption that chronological age is an accurate indicator of biological, subjective, functional and social ages.
- Burnside *et al.*'s decade-by-decade description is a way of seeing the aged as a collection of sub-groups, each with its own problems and capabilities. We need to change our stereotypes of the elderly as being needy, non-productive and unhappy.
- According to **genetic clock/programmed theory**, ageing is genetically built into every organism, whereas **accumulated damages theory** sees ageing as the result of damage due to wear-and-tear of the body during a person's lifetime. Regular

exercise can significantly reduce the deterioration of many bodily functions.

- The claim that intelligence declines fairly rapidly in old age is based on **cross-sectional studies**, which face the problem of the **cohort effect**. **Longitudinal studies** indicate that some changes in different **kinds** of intelligence appear to be age-related.

- Whilst **crystallised intelligence** increases with age, **fluid intelligence** declines for all age groups over time. This may reflect the inevitable reduction in the efficiency of neurological functioning, although we may be less often challenged to use these abilities in old age.

- Some aspects of **memory** decline with age, perhaps due to less effective information processing. Older adults **generally** perform more poorly than younger adults on recall tests, but the differences are reduced or may even disappear when recognition tests are used. Loss of cortical neurons is minimal in most humans until very late in life.

- **Negative cultural stereotypes** of ageing actually cause memory decline in the elderly and may become **self-fulfilling prophecies**.

- **Social disengagement theory** refers to the mutual withdrawal of society and the individual. Its most controversial feature is its claim that the elderly accept and even welcome disengagement and that this is a natural and **inevitable** process.

- Although there are losses in certain relationships, these are replaced to some extent by new ones. Not only is disengagement just one of many possible ways of ageing, but individuals rarely disengage from **all** roles to the same degree.

- According to **activity** or **re-engagement theory**, older people are psychologically and socially essentially the same as middle-aged people. The withdrawal of society and the individual is **not** mutual, and optimal ageing involves maintaining the activities of middle age for as long as possible.

- However, people select a style of ageing that is best suited to their **personality**, past experiences and life-style. Adjustment to old age is increasingly being seen as continuous with earlier phases of life.
- According to **social exchange theory**, there is a mainly unwritten and unenforceable **contract** between the individual and society. This involves giving up our roles as economically active members of society in **exchange** for increased leisure time and fewer responsibilities.
- Erikson's **psychosocial theory** is an example of the personal growth model. Old age involves a conflict between **ego-integrity** and **despair**. The task of ageing is to assess and evaluate life's value and meaning. Despair is characterised by a fear of death and a feeling that it is too late to undo the past and right the wrongs.

ADLER, A. (1927) *The Practice and Theory of Individual Psychology*. New York: Harcourt Brace Jovanovich.

ARGYLE, M. (1989) *The Social Psychology of Work* (2nd edition). Harmondsworth: Penguin.

ATCHLEY, R.C. (1982) Retirement: Leaving the world of work. *Annals of the American Academy of Political and Social Science*, 464, 120–131.

ATCHLEY, R.C. (1985) *Social Forces and Ageing: An Introduction to Social Gerontology*. Belmont, California: Wadsworth.

ATCHLEY, R.C. & ROBINSON, J.L. (1982) Attitudes towards retirement and distance from the event. *Research on Ageing*, 4, 288–313.

BALTES, P.B. (1987) Theoretical propositions of life-span developmental psychology: On the dynamics of growth and decline. *Developmental Psychology*, 23, 611–626.

BALTES, P.B. & BALTES, M.M. (1993) *Successful Ageing: Perspectives from the Behavioural Sciences*. Cambridge: Cambridge University Press.

BANDURA, A. & WALTERS, R. (1959) *Social Learning and Personality Development*. New York: Holt.

BARROW, G. & SMITH, P. (1979) *Aging, Ageism and Society*. St. Paul, MN: West.

BEAUMONT, P. (1996) Thirtysomethings who won't grow up. *The Observer*, 19 May, 11.

BEE, H. (1994) *Lifespan Development*. New York: HarperCollins.

BEE, H. & MITCHELL, S.K. (1980) *The Developing Person: A Lifespan Approach*. New York: Harper & Row.

BROMLEY, D.B. (1988) *Human Ageing: An Introduction to Gerontology* (3rd edition). Harmondsworth: Penguin.

BURNSIDE, I.M., EBERSOLE, P. & MONEA, H.E. (1979) *Psychological Caring Throughout the Lifespan*. New York: McGraw-Hill.

BUTLER, R. (1963) The life review: An interpretation of reminiscence in the aged. *Psychiatry*, 26, 65–76.

CAMPBELL, A. (1981) *The Sense of Well-Being in America*. New York: McGraw-Hill.

CAVANAUGH, J.C. (1995) Ageing. In P.E. Bryant & A.M. Colman (Eds) *Developmental Psychology*. London: Longman.

CHUMLEA, W. (1982) Physical growth in adolescence. In B. Wolman (Ed.) *Handbook of Developmental Psychology*. Englewood Cliffs, NJ: Prentice-Hall.

COLEMAN, J.C. (1980) *The Nature of Adolescence*. London: Methuen.

COLEMAN, J.C. (1995) Adolescence. In P.E. Bryant & A.M. Colman (Eds) *Developmental Psychology*. London: Longman.

COLEMAN, J.C. & HENDRY, L. (1990) *The Nature of Adolescence* (2nd edition). London: Routledge.

COOPER, G. (1996) The satisfying side of being home alone. *Independent*, 13 September, 3.

CRAIG, G.J. (1992) *Human Development* (6th edition). Englewood Cliffs, NJ: Prentice-Hall.

CRAMER, D. (1995) Special issue on personal relationships. *The Psychologist*, 8, 58–59.

CSIKSZENTMIHALYI, M. & LARSON, R. (1984) *Being Adolescent: Conflict and Growth in the Teenage Years*. New York: Basic Books.

CUMMING, E. (1975) Engagement with an old theory. *International Journal of Ageing and Human Development*, 6, 187–191.

CUMMING, E. & HENRY, W.E. (1961) *Growing Old: The Process of Disengagement*. New York: Basic Books.

DACEY, J.S. (1982) *Adolescents Today* (2nd edition). Glenview, Illinois: Scott, Foresman & Company.

DATAN, N., RODEHEAVER, D. & HUGHES, F. (1987) Adult development and ageing. *Annual Review of Psychology*, 38, 153–180.

DAVIES, D.L. (1956) Psychiatric illness in those enagaged to be married. *British Journal of Preventive and Social Medicine*, 10, 123–127.

DENNEY, N. & PALMER, A. (1981) Adult age differences on traditional problem-solving measures. *Journal of Gerontology*, 36, 323–328.

DIAMOND, M. (1978) Sexual identity and sex roles. *The Humanist*, March/April.

DIETCH, J.T. (1995) Old age. In D. Wedding (Ed.) *Behaviour and Medicine* (2nd edition). St Louis, MO: Mosby-Year Book.

DOOLEY, D. & PRAUSE, J. (1995) Effect of unemployment on school leavers' self-esteem. *Journal of Occupational and Organisational Psychology*, 68, 177–192.

DOWD, J.J. (1975) Ageing as exchange: A preface to theory. *Journal of Gerontology*, 30, 584–594.

DURKIN, K. (1995) *Developmental Social Psychology: From Infancy to Old Age*. Oxford: Blackwell.

DYSON, J. (1980) Sociopolitical influences on retirement. *Bulletin of the British Psychological Society*, 33, 128–130.

ELKIND, D. (1970) Erik Erikson's eight ages of man. *New York Times Magazine*, 5 April.

ENGEL, G. (1962) *Psychological Development in Health and Disease*. Philadelphia: Saunders.

ERIKSON, E.H. (1963) *Childhood and Society* (2nd edition). New York: Norton.

EYSENCK, H.J. & WAKEFIELD, J.A. (1981) Psychological factors as predictors of marital satisfaction. *Advances in Behaviour Research and Therapy*, 3, 151–192.

FOGELMAN, K. (1976) *Britain's Sixteen-Year-Olds*. London: National Children's Bureau.

FRYER, D. (1992) Signed on at the 'beroo': Mental health and unemployment research in Scotland. *The Psychologist*, 5, 539–542.

FRYER, D. (1995) Benefit agency? *The Psychologist*, 8, 265–272.

GILLIGAN, C. (1982) *In a Different Voice: Psychological Theory and Women's Development*. Cambridge, MA: Harvard University Press.

GOULD, R.L. (1978) *Transformations: Growth and Change in Adult Life*. New York: Simon & Schuster.

GOULD, R.L. (1980) Transformational tasks in adulthood. In S.I. Greenspan & G.H. Pollock (Eds) *The Course of Life: Psychoanalytic Contributions Toward Understanding Personality Development*, Volume 3: *Adulthood and the Ageing Process*. Washington, DC: National Institute for Mental Health.

GROSS, R. (1996) *Psychology: The Science of Mind and Behaviour* (3rd edition). London: Hodder & Stoughton.

HALL, G.S. (1904) *Adolescence*. New York: Appleton & Company.

HAMBURG, D. & TAKANISHI, R. (1989) Preparing for life: The critical transition of adolescence. *American Psychologist*, 44, 825–827.

HAVIGHURST, R.J. (1964) Stages of vocational development. In H. Borrow (Ed.) *Man in a World of Work*. Boston: Houghton Mifflin.

HAVIGHURST, R.J., NEUGARTEN, B.L. & TOBIN, S.S. (1968) Disengagement and patterns of ageing. In B.L. Neugarten (Ed.) *Middle Age and Ageing*. Chicago: University of Chicago Press.

HAYSLIP, B. & PANEK, P.E. (1989) *Adult Development and Ageing*. New York: Harper & Row.

HETHERINGTON, E.M. & BALTES, P.B. (1988) Child psychology and life-span development. In E.M. Hetherington, R. Lerner, & M. Perlmutter (Eds) *Child Development in Life-Span Perspective*. Hillsdale, NJ: Erlbaum.

HINTON, J. (1975) *Dying*. Harmondsworth: Penguin.

HODGSON, J.W. & FISHER, J.L. (1979) Sex differences in identity and intimacy development. *Journal of Youth and Adolescence*, 8, 37–50.

HOLAHAN, C.K. & SEARS, R.R. (1995) *The Gifted Group in Later Maturity*. Stanford, CA: Stanford University Press.

HOPSON, B. & SCALLY, M. (1980) Change and development in adult life: Some implications for helpers. *British Journal of Guidance and Counselling*, 8, 175–187.

HORN, J.L. (1982) The ageing of human abilities. In B. Wolman (Ed.) *Handbook of Developmental Psychology*. Englewood Cliffs, NJ: Prentice-Hall.

KALISH, R.A. (1982) *Late Adulthood: Perspectives on Human Development*. Monterey, CA: Brooks-Cole.

KASTENBAUM, R. (1979) *Growing Old – Years of Fulfilment*. London: Harper & Row.

KERMIS, M.D. (1984) *The Psychology of Human Ageing*. Boston: Allyn & Bacon.

KROGER, J. (1985) Separation-individuation and ego identity status in New Zealand university students. *Journal of Youth and Adolescence*, 14, 133–147.

KROGER, J. (1996) *Identity in Adolescence: The Balance between Self and Other* (2nd edition). London: Routledge.

KÜBLER-ROSS, E. (1969) *On Death and Dying*. *London*: Tavistock/Routledge.

LEVINSON, D.J. (1986) A conception of adult development. *American Psychologist*, 41, 3–13.

LEVINSON, D.J., DARROW, D.N., KLEIN, E.B., LEVINSON, M.H. & McKEE, B. (1978) *The Seasons of a Man's Life*. New York: A.A. Knopf.

LEVY, B. & LANGER, E. (1994) Ageing free from negative stereotypes: Successful memory in China and among the American deaf. *Journal of Personality and Social Psychology*, 66, 989–997.

LEVY, R. (1996) Improving memory in old age through implicit self-stereotyping. *Journal of Personality & Social Psychology*, 71, 1092–1107.

LIEBERMAN, M.A. (1993) Bereavement self-help groups: Review of conceptual and methodological issues. In M.S. Stroebe, W. Stroebe & R.O. Hansson (Eds) *Handbook of Bereavement: Theory, Research and Intervention*. New York: Cambridge University Press.

LOPATA, H.Z. (1988) Support systems of American urban widowhood. *Journal of Social Issues*, 44, 113–128.

MADDOX, G.L. (1964) Disengagement theory: A critical evaluation. *The Gerontologist*, 4, 80–83.

MARCIA, J.E. (1980) Identity in adolescence. In J. Adelson (Ed.) *Handbook of Adolescent Psychology*. New York: Wiley.

MARSLAND, D. (1987) *Education and Growth*. London: Falmer.

MAYLOR, E.A. (1994) Ageing and the retrieval of specialised and general knowledge: Performance of ageing masterminds. *British Journal of Psychology*, 85, 105–114.

McCRYSTAL, C. (1997) Now you can live forever, or at least for a century. *The Observer*, 15 June, 3.

MEILMAN, P.W. (1979) Cross-sectional age changes in ego identity status during adolescence. *Developmental Psychology*, 15, 230–231.

MILLER, E. & MORRIS, R. (1993) *The Psychology of Dementia*. Chichester: Wiley.

MONTEMAYOR, R. (1983) Parents and adolescents in conflict: All families some of the time and some families most of the time. *Journal of Early Adolescence*, 3, 83–103.

MOSER, K.A., FOX, A.J. & JONES, D.R. (1984) Unemployment and mortality in the OPCS longitudinal study. *Lancet*, 2, 1324–1329.

NEUGARTEN, B.L. (1975) The future of the young-old. *The Gerontologist*, 15, 4–9.

NEUGARTEN, B.L. & NEUGARTEN, D.A. (1987) The changing meanings of age. *Psychology Today*, 21, 29–33.

NOLLER, P. & CALLAN, V.J. (1990) Adolescents' perceptions of the nature of their communication with parents. *Journal of Youth and Adolescence*, 19, 349–362.

OFFER, D. (1969) *The Psychological World of the Teenager*. New York: Basic Books.

OFFER, D., OSTROV, E., HOWARD, K.I. & ATKINSON, R. (1988) *The Teenage World: Adolescents' Self-Image in Ten Countries*. New York: Plenum Press.

PARKES, C.M., BENJAMIN, B. & FITZGERALD, R.G. (1969) Broken heart: A statistical study of increased mortality among widowers. *British Medical Journal*, 1, 740–743.

PARKES, C.M. & WEISS, R.S. (1983) *Recovery From Bereavement*. New York: Basic Books.

PECK, R.C. (1968) Psychological developments in the second half of life. In B.L. Neugarten (Ed.) *Middle Age and Ageing*. Chicago, Ill.: University of Chicago Press.

RAMSAY, R. & de GROOT, W. (1977) A further look at bereavement. Paper presented at EATI conference, Uppsala. Cited in P.E. Hodgkinson (1980) Treating abnormal grief in the bereaved. *Nursing Times*, 17 January, 126–128.

RAPHAEL, B. (1984) *The Anatomy of Bereavement*. London: Hutchinson.

REEDY, M.N. (1983) Personality and ageing. In D.S. Woodruff & J.E. Birren (Eds) *Ageing: Scientific Perspectives and Social Issues* (2nd edition). Monterey, CA: Brooks/Cole.

RICHARDS, M.P.M. (1995) The International Year of the Family – family research. *The Psychologist*, 8, 17–20.

ROBERTS, R. & NEWTON, P.M. (1987) Levinsonian studies of women's adult development. *Psychology and Ageing*, 39, 165–174.

ROGERS, J., MEYER, J. & MORTEL, K. (1990) After reaching retirement age physical activity sustains cerebral perfusion and cognition. *Journal of the American Geriatric Society*, 38, 123–128.

RUTTER, M., GRAHAM, P., CHADWICK, D.F.D. & YULE, W. (1976) Adolescent turmoil: Fact or fiction? *Journal of Child Psychology and Psychiatry*, 17, 35–56.

RUTTER, M. & RUTTER, M. (1992) *Developing Minds: Challenge and Continuity Across The Life-Span*. Harmondsworth: Penguin.

SANGIULIANO, I. (1978) *In Her Time*. New York: Morrow.

SANTROCK, J.W. (1986) *Psychology: The Science of Mind and Behaviour*. Dubuque, IA: William C. Brown.

SARAFINO, E.P. & ARMSTRONG, J.W. (1980) *Child and Adolescent Development*. Glenview, Ill.: Scott, Foresman and Company.

SCHAIE, K.W. & HERTZOG, C. (1983) Fourteen-year cohort-sequential analysis of adult intellectual development. *Developmental Psychology*, 19, 531–543.

SCHLOSSBERG, N.K., TROLL, L.E. & LEIBOWITZ, Z. (1978) *Perspectives on Counselling Adults: Issues and Skills*. Monterey, CA: Brooks/Cole.

SELIGMAN, M.E.P. (1975) *Helplessness: On Depression, Development and Death*. San Francisco: W.H. Freeman.

SHEEHY, G. (1976) *Passages – Predictable Crises of Adult Life*. New York: Bantam Books.

SHEEHY, G. (1996) *New Passages*. New York: HarperCollins.

SIDDIQUE, C.M. & D'ARCY, C. (1984) Adolescence, stress and psychological well-being. *Journal of Youth and Adolescence*, 13, 459–474.

SIMMONS, R. & BLYTH, D.A. (1987) *Moving Into Adolescence*. New York: Aldine de Gruyter.

SIMMONS, R. & ROSENBERG, S. (1975) Sex, sex-roles and self-image. *Journal of Youth and Adolescence*, 4, 229–256.

STROEBE, M.S., STROEBE, W. & HANSSON, R.O. (1993) Contemporary themes and controversies in bereavement research. In M.S. Stroebe, W. Stroebe & R.O. Hansson (Eds) *Handbook of Bereavement: Theory, Research and Intervention*. New York: Cambridge University Press.

STUART-HAMILTON, I. (1994) *The Psychology of Ageing: An Introduction* (2nd edition). London: Jessica Kingsley.

STUART-HAMILTON, I. (1997) Adjusting to Later Life. *Psychology Review*, 4 (2), 20–23, November.

SWENSEN, C.H. (1983) A respectable old age. *American Psychologist*, 46, 1208–1221.

TANNER, J.M. (1978) *Fetus into Man: Physical Growth from Conception to Maturity*. Cambridge, MA: Harvard University Press.

TANNER, J.M. & WHITEHOUSE, R.H. (1976) Clinical longitudinal standards for height, weight, height velocity, weight velocity and stages of puberty. *Archives of Disorders in Childhood*, 51, 170–179.

TREDRE, R. (1996) Untitled article. *Observer Life*, 12 May, 16–19.

TURNBULL, S.K. (1995) The middle years. In D. Wedding (Ed.) *Behaviour and Medicine* (2nd edition). St. Louis, MO: Mosby-Year Book.

TURNER, J.S. & HELMS, D.B. (1989) *Contemporary Adulthood* (4th edition). Fort Worth, FL: Holt, Rinehart & Winston.

WARR, P.B. (1984) Work and unemployment. In P.J.D. Drenth (Ed.) *Handbook of Work and Organisational Psychology*. Chichester: Wiley.

WARR, P.B. (1987) *Work, Unemployment and Mental Health*. Oxford: Clarendon Press.

WEISS, R.S. (1993) Loss and recovery. In M.S. Stroebe, W. Stroebe & R.O. Hansson (Eds) *Handbook of Bereavement: Theory, Research and Intervention*. New York: Cambridge University Press.

INDEX

illusion of absolute safety 36
influences (on adult development)
  normative age-graded 40
  normative history-graded 40
  non-normative 40
intelligence
  crystallised **64**
  fluid **64**–5
intimacy 8, 10, 21–2, 23
isolation 22
Kalish, R.A. 59, 61
Kastenbaum, R. 60–1
Kermis, M.D. 69
Kroger, J. 12, 17
Kübler-Ross,E. 55
Langer, E. 67
Larson, R. 5–6
learned helplessness **41**
Levinson, D.J. 21, 25–30, 33, 34, 37, 40, 51
Levinson *et al.*'s. theory (early and middle adulthood) 25–34
Levy, B. 67
Lieberman, M.A. 54
life (transitions) 25–7, 28, 40
longitudinal studies 12, 64
Lopata, H.Z. 55
Maddox, G.L. 70
Marcia, J. 1, 11–12
Marcia's theory of adolescence 11–12
marker events **29**, 31, 36
marriage 46–9
Marsland, D. 13
Maylor, E.A. 65
McCrystal, C. 60
meanings of 'old' 59–62
Meilman, P.W. 12
memory in old age 65–7

mentors 28
mid-life crisis **29**, 30–2
middle adulthood 29–32
Miller, E. 65
Mitchell, S.K. 32, 63
Montemayor, R. 3–4
mood swings (in adolescence) 5–6
moratorium (adolescence as) **7**
Morris, R. 65
Moser, K.A. 43
mourning 52
National Children's Bureau, The 5, 14, 15
Neugarten, B.L. 23, 24, 71
Neugarten, D.A. 71
Newton, P.M. 33
Noller, P. 14
Offer, D. 6
old age
  memory in 65–7
  physical changes in 63
  psychological changes in 64–5
  social changes in 67–74
Palmer, A. 65
parenthood 49–51
Parkes, C.M. 52
Peck, R.C. 55–54
perceptions of ageing 59–62
perpetual adolescence 24
personal growth model (of ageing) 59
physical changes in old age 63
Prause, J. 42
psychological changes in old age 64–6
psychosocial stages of development (Erikson) 7, 8
puberty **2**–5
Ramsay, R. 52, 53, 54